LIZA D

recipe for the perfect Christmas

Gather together:
Your loving husband, Bill

your three adorable kids

Borrow sister's boyfriend

*Bribe nephews & niece
to call you Mom*

Blend with:
Your rambling
country home, all
decorated for Christmas

*Borrow sister's boyfriend's
home—promise him sister's
hand in marriage*

A delicious home-cooked
meal, featuring the
specialties of the season

*Thank God sister
can cook!*

Season with:
A real, American hero—
former hostage Jeff James,
now safely on American soil

*All six delicious,
unmarried, gorgeous
feet of him*

and:
The warmth of the Christmas season

*Or is that the warmth of looking
into Jeff's eyes . . . or the feeling
of the very hot water you're
getting into here?*

Dear Reader,

I *love* Christmas! My childhood memories are filled with images of holiday preparations in our apartment over a store in New Bedford, Massachusetts. I can see my father sitting in the middle of our pseudo-Oriental rug, a naked tree standing behind him in the bay window as he struggled with a string of lights. In those days, one faulty bulb prevented the entire string from working, and the only solution was to remove one bulb at a time and put a new one in its place. When the string still didn't light, you moved on to the next bulb. The process could take an entire evening.

My father would blame my mother for the way she'd put the lights away, and she would blame him for handling them roughly.

Even at age seven or eight, I thought it amazing that the man who'd won the Bronze Star for leading a mission behind enemy lines somewhere in Italy the year I was born could be reduced to near-hysteria by a string of lights. And that the woman who'd taken in two of her sister's children in the last year of World War II with no sure knowledge that her husband would be coming home, could threaten theatrically to run away if he didn't stop shouting and just fix the lights.

It occurred to me that I lived with two heroes who had no real concept of their accomplishments.

My parents are both gone now, but their love is with me every moment—never more vivid and more uplifting than when I prepare for Christmas.

I wish each of you the memory of past love to light your present, and the prospect of new love to brighten your future.

Muriel Jensen

P.O. Box 1168
Astoria, Oregon 97103

Muriel Jensen

CHRISTMAS IN THE COUNTRY

Harlequin Books

TORONTO • NEW YORK • LONDON
AMSTERDAM • PARIS • SYDNEY • HAMBURG
STOCKHOLM • ATHENS • TOKYO • MILAN
MADRID • WARSAW • BUDAPEST • AUCKLAND

To my readers:

Happy Holidays to all of you!

ISBN 0-373-16705-9

CHRISTMAS IN THE COUNTRY

Chapter One

"Liza, I don't care if you have to hire Martha Stewart to hide in your oven and hand food out to you," Edie Brickman shouted, "we're doing this Christmas special, and that's final!"

Liza turned away from the scene of hectic, mid-morning Manhattan visible from her apartment window and decided to try reason on her panicked editor. Particularly since yelling and screaming had gotten her nowhere.

She went across the living room toward her, mustering the easy, friendly manner that had made her *Wonder Woman Magazine* country-living articles so successful.

"Edie," she said gently, "think about it. I can't cook, I can't sew and my sister designs all those clever crafty things that I write about. You know this." Liza hooked an arm in Edie's and led her to a french blue sofa. "Do you think there will be any way I can hide that, with fifty-five minutes to fill on national television?"

Edie resisted Liza's efforts to ease her onto the

sofa. She dropped her purse on it, and her Versace coat and scarf, but her tall, coltish body remained standing, arms folded, feet slightly apart as though braced for battle.

"I got this job for you, Liza," she said, shamelessly bringing up old debts. "I thought the plan was iffy, but you were desperate for work and insisted you could pull it off." Edie waggled a finger at Liza. "I warned you that it was a recipe for trouble, but you said there was no reason it couldn't work—you wax philosophical about the cozy country life in Connecticut from your apartment in Manhattan, and your sister, who actually *does* live in rural Connecticut, provides you with the occasional recipe and craft hint that you use as your own. Okay. It was Mr. Whittier's idea that *Wonder Woman* have a country columnist, so I put you on thinking it'll make the publisher happy but it's a fad, the reader will tire of it in a year and we can move you into something else. But what do you do?"

Liza smiled flatly. "I become a sensation and quadruple your circulation. How thoughtless of me."

Edie put a hand to Liza's shoulder and pushed.

Liza fell onto the sofa and Edie sat beside her, dark eyes and severe bun making her look a decade older than her thirty-three years—and lethal. "Yes. That's what you did. But with popularity and acclaim comes responsibility—to your readers, to the magazine, to Mr. Whittier whose name is on our paychecks, but most of all..." She paused significantly. "Most of all to *me*, who put my butt on the line to get you a job and help perpetrate this charade and who is going to make you very sorry if I find myself unemployed!''

Liza leaned back against the sofa cushions, wishing desperately that there was a solution. ''Edie, I would do this if I thought there was any way I could pull it off. I mean, last year when *Wonder Woman* insisted I do that local cable show at Christmas, I got the studio set up, flew Sherrie in to help me and we made it happen, but you're talking about bringing the reader into *my* Connecticut home.''

Edie leaned back beside her, suddenly calm. ''That's right.''

They stared at the opposite wall with its family photos. ''Edie,'' Liza reminded her, ''I don't have a Connecticut home. This is where I live. Manhattan. And Sherrie can't help, either. She lives in Connecticut, but in a little duplex that not even studio lighting would make quaint.''

''Then you'll just have to find a solution, won't you?'' Edie's voice was quiet now and a little high, as though she were talking to a small child.

Liza knew what was happening. This was a sort of stabilizing technique Edie used when things got too stressful. She mentally removed herself to a peaceful distance and forced a quiet tone of voice.

Piqued because she had no such technique, Liza took pleasure in undermining Edie's.

''You said the producer also wants to feature my husband.''

''That's right.''

''And my children.''

"Yes."

"Edie, perhaps it's slipped your mind, but I don't have either—any."

Edie smiled, apparently still in her happy place. "Well, you've got about four days to acquire them."

"You know, I was thinking." Liza sat up and turned sideways, leaning an elbow on the back of the sofa as she focused on Edie. "There's another option we're not considering."

Edie rolled her head toward her on the cushion. "What's that?"

"Honesty," Liza replied.

Edie stared at her a moment, then laughed scornfully. "In publishing?" she asked. "Don't be ridiculous."

Liza sat up, warming to the idea. "I'm serious, Edie. When I took this job eighteen months ago I was desperate for work."

"And trying to help Sherrie, whose husband had just left her with two little children and another one on the way. I remember. What does that have to do with now?"

"Now I have a savings account, a little bit of fame. If I lose this job, I can get another one. And I'll even tell Mr. Whittier that I deceived you, that you never had any idea what I was doing."

Edie sat up, every muscle taut. Liza recognized her expression as the twenty-minutes-to-deadline, mess-with-me-under-pain-of-death look. "First of all, you'll get another job doing what? The fame you've acquired has been as a cozy-living, good-cooking, home-decorating, husband-loving, child-rearing columnist—the very image you're talking about destroying. Believe me, the single-woman-in-Manhattan bit just doesn't sell copy.'' Edie drew a breath. ''Secondly, I know you send a percentage of your income to help Sherrie get by. What's she going to do without it? I know she's a chef in a little gourmet restaurant in Rockbury, but she has three children to support. And thirdly…'' Edie frowned darkly, her happy place well and truly dissolved. ''Mr. Whittier will never believe I didn't know what you were doing. I have my job because nothing gets by me. You go down, girlfriend, and I go down.'' She made a chopping motion with her hand. ''In case it's not clear, we are dismissing honesty as an option.''

Liza groaned and closed her eyes. The wages of sin. Her mother had always warned her about the importance of understanding the relationship between cause and effect.

When she'd been seven and ridden on the back of nine-year-old Sherrie's toboggan, trusting blindly that her sister had checked for obstacles in their path, her mother had given them her famous speech as she tied the slings that supported their broken left arms.

''You have to look *first*,'' she'd insisted with the weary patience Liza remembered so well. Alice De Lane had been a widow who worked hard to support her daughters, and spent all her free time with them. ''Before you go off on your adventures. I know you're both very brave, but you have to apply a little common sense to your lives or you won't live long enough to enjoy the fruits of your courage.''

That hadn't made much sense then, but it did now. Sherrie had married charming, sexy Tom Blake after a six-week acquaintance—deeply, madly in love. But in the ten years they were married, he never held a job longer than three months, and finally left Sherrie for the bookkeeper in a car dealership, his last place of employment. They'd left Connecticut for a motorcycle trip across the country.

Liza had done a little job-hopping herself, though with far less frequency. She'd worked for a newspaper, an ad agency, a local television station, and as a publicity director for a design firm.

Each job had been interesting in its way, but she hadn't been able to find the stimulation and excitement she'd been so sure was out there—somewhere. And then she'd answered the ad for a country columnist for *Wonder Woman,* and the rest was history.

She'd parlayed her own dreams of the ideal life into a picture 3.7 million women believed in and wanted to emulate. And she'd found her excitement and stimulation in their response.

But now she had to deal with the fact that what she'd given them had been only her dreams and not her reality. It had all appeared so logical when she'd needed work. She and Sherrie had spent so much of their early lives helping each other that the pairing of their talents for a common purpose had seemed so natural.

It was the successful outcome of their efforts that

had become the problem. Readers loved Liza's columns about life in the country and wanted to hear more about her family, to share more of her recipes and her hints for beautifying her home with natural things.

They'd demanded a book, then a local cable special, and now they wanted her to go national, completely unaware that she was a fraud.

There *had* to be an answer, but all she could come up with was passage on a freighter to Cameroon.

The telephone rang and Liza stood listlessly, stepping over Edie's legs and going to the desk by the window. Edie's threats of retribution had apparently been toothless because she now lay sunken in the sofa, her Kate Moss legs stretched out before her, her arms flung out in an attitude of despair, probably contemplating life in the unemployment line.

Liza picked up the phone. "Hello," she said.

"Miss De Lane." It was Henry in the lobby. "There's a Mr. Whittier to see you. Do you wish to see him?"

"Ah...who, Henry?"

Liza had heard him, but she didn't believe him. So therefore she must have misunderstood.

"Whittier," Henry said again. "Benjamin Whittier. He says he's your publisher."

God! She hadn't misunderstood! She put a hand over the receiver and turned to Edie. "Mr. Whittier is here!"

"Where?" Edie came out of her thoughts, looking

around, long body drawing in as though preparing to hide.

"In the lobby!" Liza whispered. "He wants to see me! But how does he know I'm here? Everything goes to that post office box in Connecticut."

Edie came to the phone, looking frantic. "Well... he called and asked me how to reach you," she said softly, "and I gave him this phone number, telling him you kept an apartment here and that you'd come to New York to do some shopping. But I thought he was going to *call* you."

"Miss De Lane?" Henry asked worriedly.

"Send him up, Henry," Liza replied, then hung up the phone. She squared her shoulders and took Edie by hers. "Edie, I know I owe you big, but I think I'd do your career more harm than good if I tried to do this show and blew it. So I'm going to tell Mr. Whittier the truth, and I promise you I'll make sure you're in the clear."

Edie sank under her grip. "Sure. Sure. Whatever. When it's all over we'll get an apartment together somewhere in the city where cab drivers won't even go. We'll get fishnet stockings and neon-colored underwear and maybe a pimp."

Liza shook her. "Pull yourself together. Your father's a millionaire. I don't think you'll have to turn to prostitution."

"I'm going to the bathroom."

"No, you're not." Liza caught Edie's arm as she tried to retreat. "You're going to stay with me and pretend great surprise when I spill my guts, so that I can convince him you had nothing to do with this.''

Edie pulled against her. ''No. I can't lie—that's why I don't edit fiction. I'll try to say the words and my face'll get red and I'll start to stammer and he'll know! He'll know!''

''Edie!'' Liza held on. ''Listen to me. You edit me, don't you?''

''Yes.''

''And it's all a lie, isn't it?''

Edie's face crumpled.

''Okay, forget I said that. Just sit on the sofa and try to remember all those new circulation figures you were spouting at me earlier. He'll like that.''

The doorbell rang. Edie went to the sofa, a tissue pressed to her nose, and Liza went to the door, trying to decide how best to approach her employer with the news that his nationally popular country columnist couldn't boil water.

Well, she could if she had a microwave.

She pulled the door open, a cheerful greeting on her lips, but Ben Whittier didn't even hear it.

He pushed past her into the apartment, his wide, white-bearded face wreathed in smiles as he waved something in his hand.

''Edie! How fortunate that you're here, too! Wait'll you see what I've got.'' He looked around the living room, shedding his cashmere coat and tossing it at a chair. Then he grinned at Liza. ''I know you have all those farmy things to do in the country, but when you're in New York don't you watch television? Where is it?''

Liza was confused by the question, but went to the cabinet across the room and opened its double doors, revealing a television, VCR and stereo.

"Ah!" He handed her the videotape he held. "Pop that in. You won't believe this!" He sat beside Edie, waited for Liza to do as he instructed, then waved her over to sit on his other side.

Then he noticed that Edie was crying. "What's the matter?" he asked, only partially distracted.

Edie waved the tissue and said something incoherent.

"It's...the holidays," Liza said, figuring there would be plenty of time to elaborate once their boss had made his point, whatever it was.

"Well, hold on to that tissue." He picked up the remote control off the coffee table and aimed it at the television. "You're going to need it."

There was a few seconds of a group of women singing "Louie, Louie." Liza recognized one of the women as Whittier's wife. He fast-forwarded. "Sorry. My wife's sorority's talent show." Then he stopped at what appeared to be a news interview and rewound.

"...daring escape involved six days of running and hiding from Baalbek to Damascus, pursued by the Fatwa Jihad, a radical band of terrorists. Father Etienne Chabot taught French at the International School and was taken hostage in July. Jeffrey James, kidnapped in early October, came to Beirut as a consultant on a freeway project."

The camera closed in on the lined face of a small old man on a hospital gurney. He smiled weakly. *"Bonjour,"* he said, then added in heavily accented English, "Hello. Hello, Amerrrica."

"Hello, Father Chabot," the reporter said, leaning over the gurney. "How would you describe your escape from the Fatwa Jihad?" He put the mike to the priest's mouth.

"Eet was …*l'enfer,*" he said, then, smiling, translated. "Hell. Eet was hell. If it was not for *mon ami,* I would be with *le bon Dieu.*"

There was a murmur of sound as a doctor and a nurse began to push the gurney away.

"Father Chabot," the reporter said to his audience, "suffered two broken ribs and a gunshot wound to the leg in the escape. And he credits American engineer Jeffrey James with carrying him out of the line of fire and keeping him alive for six days while they evaded their pursuers and made their way over the border into Syria. Reporter Mitch Goldrick is in the American embassy in Damascus with Mr. James. Mitch?"

The scene switched to a comfortable, book-lined room and a scruffy, bearded man in a high-backed chair. The camera closed in on his face and Liza immediately rethought her impression of him as scruffy.

Thick dark brown hair was wildly unkempt and cottony looking, as though it hadn't been cared for in weeks. Lines of weariness etched his face.

But the man's eyes were remarkable. They were a vivid medium blue like the color of lobelia in a summer garden. And Liza thought the calm intelligence in them was truly extraordinary considering what he'd just been through. She wouldn't have been surprised to see in them anger for the past two months, annoyance with the reporter for intruding upon his first few hours of true freedom, thoughts of revenge, a burst of well-deserved pride in what he'd accomplished.

But she saw none of that.

"Mr. James," the reporter said, "Father Chabot says he owes you his life. What do you say to that?"

"I owe him mine, as well," Jeffrey James replied. His voice was deep, quiet. "While we were being held, he was the voice of reason to me, the touch of kindness. He made it possible for me to be chained to a chair for ten weeks and not go insane. I can't imagine how Terry Anderson dealt with being held for almost eight years."

"And that's why you brought him with you? Certainly you knew a seventy-year-old man would slow you down."

James frowned at the reporter. "I brought him with me because it would have been impossible for me to leave him there."

"He says you strapped his ribs and tended his wound."

"Actually, a kind young woman helped us."

"How did you get food?"

"She gave us some. When that ran out, I stole fruit and vegetables."

The reporter smiled. "I'll bet you're really looking forward to some good home cooking."

"I am," Jeffrey James admitted heartily.

"If you could have any dish you wanted, what would it be?"

"Apricot-glazed ham" was the instant reply.

Liza felt a little tingle along her spine. No. It couldn't be. A million women glazed ham with apricots.

"Something your mother used to make?" the reporter guessed.

James smiled and tipped his head back to lean it against the ornate chair. "No," he said with a sigh. "One of the last television shows I saw before I left for Lebanon was a Liza De Lane Christmas special. She made an apricot-glazed ham. When I was living on garbage and rice, it was all I could think of."

The tingle extended to every extremity in Liza's body.

"So, food brought you home?" the reporter teased.

James thought a moment. "No, it was more than the food. I think it was...her." He grinned wearily. "I could see her in that gingham apron, and every elemental male instinct in me identified the antiquated but still appealing concept of the nurturing woman and...I wanted her."

Liza stared openmouthed at the screen.

Edie gasped.

Whittier applauded.

"But Mr. James," the reporter said regretfully, "she's married."

Something darkened in James's eyes. Liza *knew*

she saw it. "Is she?" He shrugged philosophically and sighed. "Lucky guy."

Ben Whittier aimed the remote control at the television and the screen went black. His face was animated with excitement as he turned to Liza. "Did you *hear* that? You brought the hero home! You! *Wonder Woman*'s own Liza De Lane brought an American hostage out of two and a half months' imprisonment and provided the inspiration that helped him survive six days of terrifying danger and get himself and a comrade to safety! You, Liza. You."

Liza felt as though someone had just hit her on the head with a large mallet and shaken everything inside. As she struggled for emotional balance, all she could think about were those clear blue eyes, and the thought that the image that had led him to escape and finally to freedom had been...her.

Her in a gingham apron.

It couldn't be real. No man had ever reacted to her that way—or made her feel the way she felt now. Mushy. Vulnerable. Besotted by a pair of blue eyes.

"I've invited him to be a guest on our show," Ben said. "It'll be perfect. The last thing he saw before he left was you. Now one of the first things he'll see when Washington's finished debriefing him is you again. Liza, the ratings will go through the roof!"

Edie's horrified dark glance caught Liza's as Whittier got up to remove the tape from the VCR.

"Mr. Whittier," Edie said solemnly. "There's something we have to tell you about the show."

Ben turned away from the television at the sound

of her voice, his white eyebrows meeting in a V over the bridge of his nose. "What?"

"That we're so excited to be doing it!" Liza gushed before Edie could speak. She sent her editor a silencing look. "We have so many cozy, homey ideas that Edie gets a little emotional about it. And now that you've added a true American hero to the mix, well…" She shrugged at her inability to truly express their enthusiasm.

Ben Whittier was delighted.

Edie didn't seem to know whether to be pleased or terrified.

"Trust us, Mr. Whittier," she said. "This will be a Christmas none of us will forget."

Liza met Edie's gaze, thinking that even to her own ear the words had an unsettlingly prophetic ring.

"YOU'RE INSANE," Sherrie said. She sat across from Liza at a small table in the Rockbury Inn. Though the restaurant had just closed, Sherrie still wore her kitchen whites and chef's hat, only permed and wispy blond bangs visible under the starched band. "I told Mom you were inferior and that we should have thrown you away the moment you arrived, but she thought I was being rash. She insisted on giving you a chance. Well, I hope she's looking down on us now and admitting to herself that I was right all along."

Liza took another sip of Vouvray, then looked at her sister condemningly over the rim of the glass. "How nice of you to make this easier for me. And before you go calling people insane, you might remember who agreed to help me fill the column in the first place by providing the recipes and craft instructions that have made it so popular.''

"Because you promised to pay me.''

Liza set her stemmed glass down and, holding the rim in the tips of her fingers, gave it one turn on the tablecloth. ''Did I mention what your cut of this special would be?'' she asked casually.

Sherrie folded her arms on the table. ''Half your prison term when your boss discovers we've been deceiving him for a year and a half?''

"I don't think he'd send us to jail for quadrupling circulation. You'd make a lot of money, Sherrie.''

"How much, specifically?''

Liza named a figure that was half what she'd been offered.

Sherrie snatched the wineglass out of Liza's hand and downed the rest of the wine in one swallow. Then she put the glass down and said in a tight voice, ''Say that again.''

Liza repeated the figure, then as though the impact of it wasn't enough, she suggested its potential to change Sherrie's life. ''You could buy this place,'' she said, looking around the cozy, firelit interior of the midnineteenth-century inn. It was a wonderful place that brought to mind horse-drawn coaches, men in greatcoats and women in traveling costumes stopping for refreshment and a night's lodging. ''That's been your dream since you moved here. Now you can do it.''

Sherrie's eyes grew misty. Liza had seen that look

the night Sherrie met Tom Blake, when her children were born, and on her first day of freedom after her divorce.

Then Sherrie shook her head and leaned across the table toward Liza, the misty look overlaid by practicality. "Okay, look. I can do all the cooking for you, and you can borrow my children, since your fictitious ones are based on them, anyway. But what about the house? You said the producer wants to do outside scenes and that Mr. Whittier himself wants to be here. Where do we get the wonderful Federal mansion all your readers think you write from?"

Liza leaned toward her sister, thinking that Sherrie was one of the smartest, bravest women she knew, but a complete conehead where men were concerned.

"You really don't recognize it?" Liza asked.

Sherrie's brow furrowed in confusion. "Of course I don't recognize it. You live in a Manhattan highrise."

"And you have no idea where I got the dining room with the Pennsylvania walnut harvest table, the five-foot-tall brick fireplace, the stenciled borders on the walls, the tall-case country clock…" Liza stopped when Sherrie continued to look blank. "It's *Bill's* house, sis. When I dreamed up my fictitious house for the column, I just mentally moved into Bill McBride's house."

Sherrie sat up, stiffening. "No," she said simply.

Liza had been dealing with her for thirty years. She knew precisely what to do. "Okay," she said amiably, pulling her wallet out of the envelope bag at her feet. "You're probably right. It is insane. I just thought I'd run it by you and see what you thought."

She put several bills on the little silver salver that held her tab.

Sherrie picked up the bills and put them back in front of Liza. "I can't ask Bill to let us use his house," she said firmly. "I've been fending him off for a year, and it would send the wrong message."

Liza put the money back. "I understand. It's okay. Really."

"But what'll you do?"

"That's my problem." She smiled so that she didn't sound self-pitying. "There must be another house around here I can use."

"What if there isn't?"

Liza shrugged as though it didn't matter. "I simply tell Mr. Whittier the truth. I fully intended to do that until he came over with that video of Jeffrey James."

Sherrie sighed and stared at the inn's proprietor, a rotund little Italian man with graying hair, as he moved around the dining room, gathering tablecloths into bundles for the laundry and upturning chairs onto the tables to prepare to vacuum the burgundy carpet.

"Liza," she said, focusing on her again, her eyes anxious and a little desperate. Liza understood her sister's anguish, but she didn't think *she* did. "I can't be near him for the time it would take...."

"I know." Liza stood and pulled on her red wool coat. "It's hard to be around a man you love but are determined not to marry."

Sherrie stood, too, an inch taller than Liza. "I don't

love him. How many times do I have to tell you that? He's just the kids' pediatrician. And even if I did love him, I wouldn't put myself through marriage again. I like dealing with my children the way *I* think is right. I like knowing I can meet my budget because nobody else is siphoning off the bottom. I like going up to bed without worrying about finding my man there with another woman—because there *is* no man there.''

''Of course. I understand.''

''Liza, I've just gotten Bill to stop calling. Mercifully the kids have cooperated by being healthy, and I haven't even had to see him professionally in two months!''

Liza took Sherrie into her arms and hugged her tightly. ''Thanks for taking the time to listen. You know I've always appreciated that about you. I'll be down Christmas Day just like we...''

Sherrie held her away and glared at her. ''I hate it when you pretend I'm not talking!''

Liza blinked innocently. ''What do you mean?''

Sherrie dropped her hands and turned away, then spun back and whipped off her hat. Long blond hair the color of candlelight fell to her shoulders. ''You know what I mean,'' she admonished. ''You pretend to humor me and all the while your secret agenda is to make me change my mind. Well, fine! I'll do it!'' And she stormed behind the bar to the telephone.

It took Liza several seconds to realize she'd won. She did her best not to look self-satisfied when her sister reappeared, pulling on a thick blue parka.

Sherrie marched past her toward the door. "I'm doing this for the inn and for you," she said. "And not because I want to see Bill. Come on. He's still up. Good night, Denio."

The man paused in his work to blow a kiss.

This should be interesting, Liza thought. She couldn't wait to see Sherrie's reaction when she told her she intended to ask Bill to play the part of *Mr.* De Lane.

Chapter Two

Jeffrey James lay in the middle of an enormous bed in the penthouse suite of the Washington Regent Hotel listening to the subtle night sounds of Washington, D.C. The room was being paid for by Whittier Publications, and Ben Whittier himself was coming in a limo for him in the morning to take him to Liza De Lane's home in Connecticut.

He wished he'd kept his mouth shut about the apricot-glazed ham. That was what happened when a man got chatty. He talked himself into things that were better left alone. But he'd been on embassy soil after six days of being sure he'd never make it, and he'd been a little intoxicated with success.

That was how he'd gotten kidnapped in the first place. He'd defended the United States in an argument on the job and was taken for a spy.

Most religious and political fanatics had stopped taking hostages years earlier because they'd eventually realized there was little to gain by it. But the Fatwa Jihad were young and wild and thought the old lessons didn't apply to them.

And that was just about the way his luck had been running.

He'd left Los Angeles so that he could have something else to think about after his breakup with Sylvia. Well, that had certainly happened. After nine months of overseeing the building of a freeway in heat that fused your eyelids together, he was kidnapped and tied to a chair where he was able to do nothing *but* think for the next ten weeks.

Then he fought his way to freedom under extremely difficult conditions, and looked for some single image to sustain him in his moments of despair. The most powerful image he could think of was that of a woman, but he didn't have one. Sylvia had left him for a Dallas rancher.

So he distilled his vision of the American woman in general into the image of Liza De Lane—the woman who'd created that mouthwatering ham he'd caught a glimpse of on his way through Sylvia's place to pick up the boots he'd left in a corner of her closet.

He remembered clearly that he'd hesitated in the doorway, captivated by an oval face topped with upswept golden blond hair and cocoa brown eyes that glistened from Sylvia's television set.

She'd had pink cheeks, lips a bright fire-engine color that had caught his eye and made him focus on the shape of every word she spoke. And she'd been wearing a red-and-white gingham apron. He knew it made him a politically incorrect macho warthog, but he'd found it all a total turn-on.

Thinking back, he guessed it was because there'd

been so little softness in his life at that moment, and she represented for him something irretrievably lost—and in typical warthog fashion, he lusted for it.

And *now* they tell him she's married.

And then they invite him to spend Christmas with her in Connecticut—with her husband and children.

When he'd operated his own engineering firm before he'd left for Beirut, he'd had an office manager. He wondered if there was such a thing as a life manager. He understood that God was supposed to be in charge of that, but he and God hadn't been very close since he stopped going to Sunday school in the fifth grade.

Jeff closed his eyes and sighed. Maybe that was why his life was such a wreck. God had it in for him for abandonment.

IN THE FOUR DAYS since Bill had agreed to let Liza take over his home as her own from the twenty-first of December through Christmas Eve, Sherrie had done a masterful job of decorating the interior. Liza stood in the middle of the living room and looked around in awe.

Dora, Bill McBride's housekeeper, took Liza's bags. "Sit down, Miss De Lane...." She paused to hunch her plump shoulders and grin conspiratorially. "I mean, *Mrs. McBride*...and I'll tell your *husband* you're here." She went off toward the kitchen, giggling.

Looking around, Liza realized, not for the first

time, that her sister was a creative genius. Sherrie had brought Christmas to the country, big-time.

When Bill McBride had bought and redecorated the house five years earlier, he'd restored important architectural details such as the wooden mantel and the small-paned windows.

Now, with a fire in the fireplace and the soft light of evening warming the creamy white walls and the stenciled borders under the crown molding, Liza half expected some wealthy merchant in colonial garb to walk down the maple stairway, his arms loaded with packages.

Sherrie had decorated the mantel with pine boughs and tall candlesticks with red tapers. Pine garlands, hung at intervals with wooden bird ornaments, were strung along the stairway's balustrade.

A red, green and white quilt was thrown over the back of a sofa upholstered in a brick red color sprinkled with tiny cream dots. A matching wing chair stood on one side of the fireplace, and another wing chair in a coordinating pattern occupied the other side.

A small quilt throw covered a low table before the sofa, and on it was a white teapot and a plate of cookies.

Liza had sent Sherrie all the family portraits that decorated her wall in the apartment in Manhattan, and her sister had placed them above the fireplace, using a large, ornately framed photo of their great-grandparents' wedding as the centerpiece.

Liza choked.

She felt emotion swell in her chest, close her throat, fill her eyes, and she couldn't explain it precisely, unless it was guilt that she'd brought all these loving people from her past into her holiday play. All the smiling faces who'd passed love down the generations now looked down on her and probably wondered what in the hell she was doing.

She sniffed, swallowed and patted her hair. She knew what she was doing. She was getting Sherrie the money to buy the inn, saving Edie's job, and...and making Ben Whittier happy.

But what was she doing for herself?

She knew that, too. She was giving herself the opportunity to meet the man who'd seen her on television and used her face as an icon in a dark hour to get himself home.

She trembled just a little at the knowledge that she'd had that effect on someone.

She turned as she caught sight of glowing color in her peripheral vision and saw what had to be the tallest, fattest, most perfectly shaped Christmas tree in the entire world. And it had been decorated with gaudy splendor.

There were hundreds of colorful lights on it, garlands of popcorn and cranberries alternately strung, traditional glass balls, wooden ornaments, tin and crystal ornaments to catch and reflect the light, and it was topped by a tall, lacy angel who held a candle whose flame was also a light. The area under the bottom boughs was stacked with brightly wrapped presents.

"My…God!" Liza breathed, stunned by the magnificence of it.

"Liza." A hand fell gently on her shoulder and she turned to see Bill McBride standing behind her. He was a tall, thickly built man in his early forties with thick dark hair graying at the temples, expressive brown eyes and a ready smile. He wore casual gray slacks and a blue, gray and white plaid shirt. "Some tree, huh?"

Liza still couldn't quite believe it. "It's magnificent. The whole room is."

"Wait till you see the rest of the house," Bill said, his gaze focused on the tree. "I like to think that this reflects some deep personal need of her own. That she would do it just this way if she lived here."

Liza wanted to think so, too, but she liked Bill. She hated the thought of her sister hurting him.

"I admit that when I came up with this idea," she said as he helped her off with her coat, "I thought about what this could do for the two of you. Proximity is always a catalyst for resolution—one way or the other. But…"

She waited while he took her coat to the guest closet and hung it up.

"But she's adamant about staying single," Liza continued as he led her toward the kitchen. "Tom put her through hell at the end and she's determined to enjoy her freedom."

He stopped at the doorway, nodding. "She's told me that over and over. But when the two of you came over that night to propose your plan to me, I thought she looked a little upset when you asked me to play the role of your husband.''

She smiled over that forgotten detail. "She did, didn't she?"

"She did. I take that as a good sign."

"But she could be jealous of you and still refuse to marry you."

He sighed with forbearance. "True. But I'm using reverse psychology on her now." He grinned. "I've had the courses. Pediatrics—dealing with the parents, anyway—is a step above practicing psychiatry without a license. After a year of pleading with her to marry me and being rejected, I've spent the past two months ignoring her."

"She told me. Only she made it sound like she was ignoring you."

"I guess that's true, too, only she did have Travis call me and ask me if I was spending Thanksgiving alone."

"Were you?"

He winced, as though from a painful memory. "I was. But I was determined to keep my distance until she closes the gap and comes to me. So I told her I was going to my sister's in Vermont. Then I had to leave town so she wouldn't know I'd lied."

Liza put a sympathetic hand to his arm. "Where did you go?"

"Mystic. All by myself."

Liza nodded. The historic old seaport town was a wonderful place. "At least it's beautiful there."

"Yeah," he said grimly. "But beauty seems to hurt

when you see it alone. Come on. You won't believe this kitchen.''

They passed through the dining room, which was also painted a creamy white, but here the woodwork had been painted a deep rose and the stenciling had been done in spruce green and a lighter rose.

The long, narrow sawbuck table bore a strip of pine boughs down the middle. Tall candlesticks were interspersed.

Above the table a rough, ironwork chandelier with crenellated cups holding a dozen candles was also hung with boughs.

"Silk, flame-retardant boughs," Bill explained.

A rough corner cupboard in its original milk-paint had a basil-and-strawflower wreath on its door.

Liza could just imagine Ben Whittier's delight when he arrived the following day with Jeffrey James.

Bill's kitchen had a five-foot brick fireplace that took up an entire wall. Liza often used descriptions of it in her columns. She told her readers she rocked her baby by it when she awoke during the night, and that her boys played near it on cold winter afternoons.

Sherrie had made a garland of pine, apples, oranges and gourds and attached it to the old wooden plank that marked the top of the bricks. Under the garland she'd hung long, knit stockings and she'd stenciled names on each. Betsy, Davey, Travis, Liza and Bill.

"I'm fantasizing," Bill said as Liza put a hand to her heart at the realistic touch Whittier would certainly notice, "that she made one with her name on

it and has stashed it in the bottom of a drawer some-
place.''

Liza drew a steadying breath. "I hope so."

In a little alcove in the kitchen Sherrie had placed
all the old toys she'd collected for her children, and
strewn them around a table on which she'd placed a
small Christmas tree decorated with gingerbread
cookies.

Against another wall an old iron woodstove held a
huge, brightly polished copper kettle, and canned
fruits stood on the top shelf looking like jars of
jewels, along with a kerosene lamp and a wire basket
filled with eggs.

A dry sink cupboard on another wall had an open
door that revealed more preserves, tin plates, a coffee
mill and old pottery jugs, one of which held a sprig
of glossy holly. Sherrie had hung a holly wreath on
the inside of the open door.

On the long kitchen table a collection of containers
was grouped in the middle. A tray held shiny red
apples with a flickering candle in a votive cup. A clay
pot held sand that supported a tall candle; a glass vase
held three white roses, and visible in the water that
held them was the unexpected touch of gleaming red
radishes. There were cranberries in a glass bowl with
another votive light in the middle of them.

"She must have worked twenty-four hours a day
for the last four days," Liza said, thinking very seriously that she should simply hand the column over
to her sister. She was obviously 126 pounds of un-
tapped genius.

"Almost." Bill looked around, shaking his head. "And she had Dora and the boys and me working, too. By the second night I was praying for a 2:00 a.m. call from an anxious parent that would turn out to be nothing but would allow me to find a tavern that was open all night."

Liza laughed. "You know, if she does end up accepting your many proposals, you'll be subjected to this kind of thing all the time."

He smiled wistfully. "But then, I'd have her in my arms when it was all over, wouldn't I?"

"Hold that thought, Bill." Liza could think of nothing she'd like better than having Bill McBride as a brother-in-law. And permanent access to this house. "Where is she, anyway?"

Bill glanced at his watch. "She took the boys to caroling practice, and she was going to stop by the inn to make sure they took her off the schedule through Christmas. Apparently they have a lot of bookings for the holiday." The big brass kettle spouted steam, and he went to the stove to turn it off. He opened a cupboard door. "Earl Grey tea still your favorite?"

"Yes," she replied, pulling a chair out at the long table. "Me and Captain Picard. But you don't have to wait on me. I'll be disturbing your life sufficiently over the next few days."

He brought her a mug of tea and a saucer for the bag, then sat at the head of the table with a cup of coffee.

"Happy to oblige. It's my last chance with Sherrie."

Liza drew the tea bag back and forth across the cup. "Why your last chance?"

"She intends to buy the inn with what she makes on the show. She's already spoken to Denio about it." He stared into his cup with a fatalistic expression. "She won't need me to provide security for her and the kids. She'll be able to do it herself."

Liza straightened in surprise. "Bill," she said, "that was *never* what attracted her to you."

"I know, but it was what forced her to communicate with me. She had to call me to ask me to be patient about her bill. I'd have torn it up in a minute, but it kept her in contact with me. Then when she saw this article about stenciling in a magazine in my waiting room and asked me if she could make a copy of it, I saw another opportunity and hired her to stencil the living room and dining room." He smiled in memory. "That was great. I had her for a couple of hours every evening. She was on a ladder and I was pretending to ignore her, but she was in my house. Then I had her cater a few parties for me. I hate parties, but again, it brought her into the house because she needed the money. God. That woman in a white shirt and bow tie makes me wild."

"Well, she needs more than money from you. I think that's why she's so adamant about not getting involved. She knows you're what she needs, but she doesn't want to give up her freedom."

The doorbell rang melodically through the house.

Liza frowned when Bill didn't get up to answer it.

"It's Sherrie," he said with a rueful smile. "I've given her a key, and she and the kids have been living here for the past few days, but she doesn't want me to think she's settled in or anything, so she rings the bell before she comes in, no matter how many times a day she comes and goes."

Liza smiled. "Did I mention that she's the stubborn one?"

"No kidding."

Liza's nephews exploded into the kitchen, both blond and blue-eyed in heavy green-and-gray stadium-style jackets.

"Aunt Liza!" Davey, eight, launched himself around the table and into her arms. "Hi! Mom says we're all gonna be on television!"

"That's right." She hugged him to her. His jacket was cold and he smelled of the fragrant winter. His cheeks were apple red, his eyes bright with excitement. "You think you'll like that?"

He nodded, then frowned. "If I don't forget. I have to call you 'Mom,' Bill 'Dad' and Mom 'Aunt Sherrie.' That's gonna be weird."

"But it's going to get us new bikes, right? Hi, Aunt Liza." Travis, ten, leaned around his brother to hug her.

"Right," Liza replied, thinking that he must have grown three or four inches since she saw him for his birthday in August. "That's the bribe. The bike of your choice for a good performance."

"Cool. Would that include a motorcycle?"

"No way."

"Just asking."

Sherrie shouldered her way into the room, a bag of groceries in one arm, a plump, blond baby in a pink snowsuit in the other. Liza stood to take the baby. Betsy shrank from her and screamed.

"What *is* it with this child?" Liza demanded as she sat down again, totally rebuffed. "She's hated me from the moment you brought her home from the hospital."

Bill rose instantly to take the baby from her.

"Thank you," Sherrie said with a quick, smiling glance at Bill. "You were my Lamaze coach, Liza. She probably doesn't trust you after you cajoled her down that path."

"Well, this is going to look great to my viewing audience."

Bill laughed. "Don't worry. I'll hold her when I'm around. She likes me."

The baby kicked and gave Bill a broad smile displaying two bottom teeth, obviously comfortable with him. That should be no surprise, Liza thought, since he was her pediatrician. And he handled her with the ease of long experience, sitting down again and placing her on his knee while he held her with one hand and expertly extricated her from the snowsuit with the other.

The boys went to Bill, Travis resting an elbow on his shoulder, Davey leaning against his other side.

"So, Pop," Travis said. "Can we have a raise in our allowances?" He had his father's good looks, and had also inherited his perpetual exploitation of the proverbial angle. He was always after something. Fortunately, he'd also been born with his mother's inherent goodness and sense of responsibility.

Bill handed him the baby's snowsuit. "You can't even expect your usual allowance if you call me 'Pop.'"

"But Dad's 'Dad,'" Travis said without any evidence of emotional trauma, but with an unexpectedness that brought up every adult head. "I'm not going to call you 'Father,' and we can't call you 'Bill.'"

Liza saw Bill's eyes meet Sherrie's over the baby's head and wondered why it had never occurred to her that the boys might find some difficulty in pretending that another man was their father, even for a brief few days. Some mother material she was.

"You're right," Bill said easily. "Pop it is. But no raise in allowance until I see what a good actor you are."

"I'll be great," Travis promised. "Don't worry. It's Davey you have to worry about."

"I can be great, too," Davey said with quiet lack of conviction. "If I don't forget."

Liza felt a little constriction of guilt in her chest and went to wrap her arms around her youngest nephew. He was sweet and sensitive and worried about everything. "If you do forget, nothing terrible will happen, so don't worry."

"We won't be on television if I forget."

"Sure we will." We'll just be humiliated and then fired. "All we have to do is look like one big happy family. If it's easier for you, just don't use names. Then you won't say the wrong one. But even if you do, it'll be okay."

He looked relieved.

Sherrie glanced at the clock as she put away groceries. "You guys go take your showers," she instructed. "It's getting late. Call me when you're ready to be tucked in."

"Already?" Davey whined.

Travis waved him to follow. "Come on. We'll look through the Sears catalog and pick out bikes."

"Yeah!" Galvanized into action, Davey followed Travis. Their thundering footsteps could be heard on the stairs.

"I'm sorry," Liza said to Sherrie, getting up to make her a cup of tea. "I never gave a thought to the dad thing. They've seemed so unaffected by the fact that Tom's gone."

Sherrie folded the paper bag, her expression philosophical. "He was never that great with them, but I know they kept hoping he would suddenly turn around and notice them, see how wonderful they are. But he was always too important to himself to notice us."

"They're probably just not comfortable with the idea of elbowing him aside altogether by making someone else 'Dad.'" Bill stood, Elizabeth riding his hip, went to the cupboard and took down a box of animal crackers. "This way they can compartmentalize us. Tom's 'Dad,' and I'm 'Pop.' Kids can be very clever at solving their problems. Adults should be as good.''

Liza thought the remark was innocently made, but Sherrie's head turned in his direction, her eyes suspicious. He went through the swinging door without a backward look, saying something about checking with his answering service.

Sherrie tossed her hair and put the bag away in a rack in the utility closet. ''I hope we know what we're doing,'' she said, accepting the cup of tea Liza handed her. ''This is starting to feel just a little scary to me.''

''Nonsense,'' Liza said bracingly, sweeping a hand around the beautifully decorated kitchen. ''You've done such an amazing job I'm seriously thinking I should just turn the column over to you.''

Sherrie rolled her eyes and sipped at her tea, leaning back against the counter. ''That's why we agreed to do this in the first place. I have the homemaking know-how, but you're the one with the communication skills. Even your grocery lists are exciting. You're the one who makes life in the Connecticut countryside seem so real to those big-city people who read you. I don't understand things, I just...try to beautify them. Only, some redecorating tricks just don't stick, no matter how hard you try.''

Liza leaned against the counter beside her. ''Like life with Tom?''

''Yes.''

''Sometimes you can't redecorate, you have to renovate. Knock down and start over.''

"Maybe sometimes you should just leave well enough alone."

"But life keeps moving. We have to, too."

Sherrie turned to her, her blue eyes reproachful. "You know, for someone who leaves herself little time to do anything else but work, you certainly have a lot of advice for me. Have you noticed that *you're* not moving anywhere? Oh, sure, your career is, but your life isn't. How long has it been since your last date?"

Liza went to the kettle to pour more hot water over the tea bag in her cup. "Too long. In fact, that's...sort of why we're here."

Sherrie looked confused. "I've missed something."

Liza went to her purse, removed the videotape of Jeffrey James and handed it to Sherrie. She put it in the TV-VCR mounted on the wall and watched silently as the man talked about Liza and how thoughts of her had gotten him through his difficult escape.

Liza had watched the tape over and over and now knew the words by heart.

"Lucky guy," James said in response to the reporter's revelation that she was married.

The interview over, Sherrie reached up to turn off and eject the tape. She handed it to Liza, her eyes wide with astonishment.

"But...sis. There's a major flaw here," she said. "You are going to get to meet him, but he's going to think you have a husband and three children!"

This was true. The situation was complicated, to

say the least. But she wasn't going to miss meeting him and spending time with him.

She put the tape back in her purse and sank into a chair. "This is one of those adventures Mom warned us about, where we should have looked both ways."

Sherrie sat beside her, grinning. "We? As I remember it, I was cooking at the inn, minding my own business, and you invited me into the dining room to share a bottle of wine and dragged me into this."

Liza challenged her with a look. "And you didn't *want* to spend three days here with Bill."

Sherrie looked away. "No, I didn't." She looked back again. "But I would like to own the inn. So there. I admit I'm not blameless. But how does that help you?"

Liza smiled grimly. "It means we'll get mowed down by our adventure together."

"Oh, good."

Chapter Three

"Here we are!" Ben Whittier pointed through the window of the limo as it turned off the road and through an entrance in a low stone wall onto an oak-lined drive. The trees were bare limbed and ancient against a stormy sky.

At the head of the drive Jeffrey James could see a slate blue Federal-style house with gray shutters and two dormer windows on a third level. There was a fanlight window above a wide oak door on which hung a fat green wreath with a red bow. White lights trimmed the door and the window.

He allowed himself a sigh. He'd imagined a low, rambling farmhouse rather than the formality of this three-story structure.

Whittier beamed. "Imagine how that's going to look to the camera as it sweeps slowly up the drive. History and country hospitality all warmly wrapped in one pretty package. That's our Liza."

Jeff smiled to himself. Her appeal for him had been far more basic than that, but now that he knew she was married, he would have to concentrate on her skill as the doyenne of country life rather than on those beautifully formed red lips that he could see every time he closed his eyes.

"We're a couple of hours early," Whittier said, frowning as the limo drew closer to the house. "When we got out of that interview so much earlier than I expected, it seemed logical to take the earlier flight. I hope they're home. Well, no matter. There are worse places to wait than in a warm limo with sherry and a television set."

Jeff saw that there were no lights on in the house, at least on this side of it, and the sky threatened snow, making it dark for early afternoon.

Jeff hoped for a blizzard. So often during his long, hot siege in Beirut he'd dreamed of snow falling on his face, into his mouth, down his collar.

The limo driver pulled up in front of what appeared to be a coach house that had probably been turned into a garage. Whittier climbed out and went up to the door.

Jeff got out also, slightly claustrophobic after the long drive with the effusive Whittier. It wasn't that he didn't appreciate enthusiasm in someone, just that his mind was still so cluttered with all the fuss of his homecoming that he longed for a moment alone.

He walked around the back of the house, where a good half acre of wintry lawn stretched toward more stone wall. A ladder was propped up against an oak tree, and a small man in a big, grubby coat and a stocking cap was cutting something from it.

He went to the ladder and tugged on the hem of the coat. "Pardon me," he said. "I'm looking for..."

That was as far as he got. It occurred to him later that he should have known better than to startle someone atop a ladder, but he'd thought the man was old, judging by the age and condition of the coat, and that he probably wouldn't move very fast.

But he'd been wrong on all counts.

There'd been a sudden graceful but overbalanced turn, the bounce of a basket off his shoulder as the pruner lost control of it and dropped it, a little scream of alarm, then the coat and what it contained toppled backward into his arms.

Jeff knew instantly that it was not a man. And it was not old.

His tight grasp on the body left him with one hand fastened on a round breast, and the other arm wrapped around the soft curve of a female derriere. Shocked brown eyes he recognized instantly looked up at him as Liza De Lane's hands clung to his shoulders for support.

For an instant he forgot all the promises he'd made to himself and was tempted to react with a style and stoutheartedness befitting the setting. He had no horse to fling her onto, but he could put her into the limo and drive off with her. And he got the strangest impression, from the softening in her eyes as she seemed to recognize him, that she wouldn't mind.

"Jeff? What are you doing? Who is that?" Whittier's voice came from somewhere behind him.

Liza looked over his shoulder at her publisher and began to struggle.

With a grim sense of acceptance, Jeff set her on her feet. She was smaller than he had thought, or maybe it was just the length of the ratty old coat that seemed to shrink her from the lively woman he'd seen on television.

"Well." Whittier looked from one to the other with satisfaction. "That's one way to eliminate small talk. Liza, I'd like you to meet Jeffrey James. Jeff, this is your hostess, Liza De Lane."

She pulled off a thick canvas glove and offered him a small, slender hand. "Mr. James," she said, the formal voice at odds with the look he'd seen in her eyes a moment ago. "You never stop being a hero, do you?"

He brought her knuckles to his lips. "I had a Southern mother and a military father," he replied. "I never had a chance. Please call me Jeff."

Several people suddenly burst from the back door of the house, a tall man in cords and a flannel shirt in the lead.

"Liza!" he said, coming to a stop in front of her, his eyes dark with concern, his hands molding her shoulders, tracing down her arms. He seemed surprised to find her sound. "Davey said you fell off the ladder."

"I did." She smiled and indicated Jeff with her bare hand. "But Jeffrey James caught me. Jeff, this is my husband, Bill McBride. Bill, these are our guests, Jeff James, our hero, and Ben Whittier, my boss. Mr. Whittier, my husband, Bill. Boys?''

Two young towheads came forward. He guessed them to be close to the same age, nine and ten, maybe. They bore a strong resemblance to her.

''Jeff, Mr. Whittier, these are our boys, Davey—'' she tapped the head of the younger one ''—and Travis.''

Travis shook Jeff's hand, then Davey followed his example.

''Did you have a gun when you escaped?'' Travis asked him, wide-eyed.

''No,'' he replied. ''No gun.''

''A knife?''

''No. ''

''Nunchakus?''

Jeff couldn't resist a laugh, but ruffled the boy's hair so he wouldn't think he was laughing at him. ''I don't think anybody really owns nunchakus outside of Chuck Norris movies. No. All I had was a real desire to get out of there.''

''Trav.'' Liza De Lane pulled the boy into her arm. ''Jeff's probably done all the talking he wants to do on that subject to reporters. He's come here to rest and relax.''

Travis grinned at him. ''So maybe we can talk about it later?''

Jeff nodded. ''Sure.''

Liza waved a dark, plump, white-aproned woman forward. ''This is Dora, our housekeeper.''

He offered his hand. ''Hello, Dora.''

"And this is my sister, Sherrie Blake, who'll be helping me get the food together for the show." Liza gestured a young woman toward her. Sherrie resembled Liza, but her manner seemed quieter, more reserved. In her arms was a baby girl who smiled at him, then hid her face in the woman's shoulder. "And the coy one is Elizabeth. Betsy, actually."

"Hi, Betsy." Jeff gently poked the baby's back.

She turned to him and studied him with grave blue eyes.

He held his hands out to her. She studied him uncertainly another moment, then reached for him.

"Well," Sherrie said in surprise.

Jeff settled the baby comfortably against him. "I'm pretty good with babies," he boasted. "I have friends in Beirut who have three little girls. Before I was taken, I saw them a lot."

"You have no family missing you for Christmas?"

He shook his head, adjusted to the fact. "Not a soul. Thank you for inviting me."

Ben Whittier rubbed his hands together. "Can we get this man inside and pour something warm down him? And possibly down me, too?"

"Of course. I'm sorry." Liza took the baby from Jeff and quickly handed her to the older boy, then hooked an arm in Whittier's and one in Jeff's and followed her family and the housekeeper toward the back door of the house. "I have mulled apple cider," she said. "And a gingerbread just ready to come out of the oven."

Bill McBride headed for the limo. "I'll get your

bags. And I'll bet your driver could use a glass of something hot.''

Whittier looked startled. "The driver? Oh, yeah. Sure.''

Jeff followed Liza into the warm, fragrant room and experienced the feeling he'd been waiting for since he'd stepped off an air force plane onto American soil almost a week ago. He was home.

Not that he'd ever known a home like this one. His parents had been very middle class, always struggling to make ends meet. But they'd been happy, and the kitchen had always smelled of something good.

He'd lost them both when he was in college, but he'd been so busy working at night to stay in school that he hadn't had time to concentrate on his grief or his loneliness.

But other people's homes always reminded him of what he was missing. He'd felt it every time he walked into his friend Abdul's house—the warmth, the energy, the healing serenity that love brought, even under the chaos of a dozen voices talking at once.

This kitchen was huge and smelled of something spicy—the gingerbread, he guessed. A fire danced in a large fireplace, and the flick of a switch brought light to burnish copper pieces of cookware, the chrome on an old stove, a glass vase filled with roses and...radishes?

He didn't know why, but that made him smile.

The housekeeper went to the oven and pulled the

door open, filling the room with an even stronger, more tantalizing aroma.

Sherrie pulled out a chair for him, handed his jacket to the younger boy, then went to the counter where Liza was taking dishes out of a cupboard.

A slightly startled liveried limo driver walked into the kitchen, sweeping off his hat to reveal a shiny bald head. Liza's husband followed him in with a suitcase in each hand and one tucked under his arm.

Liza turned away from the counter, drew the driver to a chair opposite Jeff and pushed on his shoulder until he sat.

Jeff and the driver had gotten acquainted while Whittier had stopped in at the *Wonder Woman* office on their way out of town. He knew the man had two sons at Boston College, and that he'd catered to the traveling whims of the rich and famous his entire life to get them there. His name was Hartman.

"I don't usually get invited in," Hartman said to Jeff under his breath. "I feel like a bull in a china shop."

Liza, bringing a tray with steaming mugs on it to the table, overheard him. She put one mug in front of him, one before Mr. Whittier and one in front of Jeff. "No china here, Mr....?"

"Hartman."

"Mr. Hartman. These are pottery, so no need to worry. Gingerbread?"

"Please."

"Whipped cream?"

"Yes. Thank you."

"Mr. Whittier?"

"Yes, please, Liza."

"Jeff?"

Jeff looked up into her eyes and felt the atmosphere around him change. Everything faded from view but her, and it felt as though they were in a vacuum together, breathing each other's air.

She'd shed the big coat and cap and looked like a Christmas flower in a roll-necked red sweater and pants. Her hair was loose and full like strands of sunshine, almost straight but curling under at the ends just above her shoulders.

Her eyes were the color of the spicy cider, and her smile made up for ten long weeks of near despair.

He let himself absorb the warmth of her until he saw the sudden shift of discomfort in her eyes and realized what he was doing. Though he'd been through hell and a half, she was not a bonus he was entitled to because he'd survived. She was married to another man—and a nice guy, by all indications. He had to remember that.

"Gingerbread, please," he said, forcibly pulling himself back from their little bubble of isolation. "But no whipped cream."

"Right." She turned away, a little frown between her eyebrows.

God. She'd invited him to be her guest, and here he was staring at her and probably making her wonder what kind of lunatic she'd brought into her home.

With a minimum of fuss everyone was served, including Bill, who'd returned, and the boys, who eyed the rich dark cake greedily.

While they ate, Whittier talked about the format for the show scheduled to be aired live Christmas Eve. "The crew will arrive in the morning to set up," he said, "and we'll go on the air at eight. We'll introduce your family, then Jeff, then we'll give a brief tour of your home. After that we'll show some film we'll tape that morning of the grounds and the countryside, then we'll do a brief interview with Jeff, devoting the second half hour entirely to your Christmas dinner."

Liza smiled—a little thinly, Jeff thought. She was bouncing the now-fussing baby on her knee. "Sounds good," she said. "You ready for this, too, Sherrie?"

"Absolutely," Sherrie replied.

The baby stretched her pudgy little hands toward Liza's hot cider, then screamed when Liza moved the cup out of her reach.

Liza spooned up a little bit of whipped cream to put to Betsy's mouth, but the baby pushed it away, her little voice picking up volume.

Liza, looking harassed, turned to her sister, who seemed to be watching her struggles with the baby with interest.

Bill walked around the table and reached down for the baby. "Here, Liza. Let me have her so you can talk. I think it's naptime."

Liza handed Betsy up to him. "Thank you, darling," she said.

When Bill disappeared, Whittier looked around the

warm, cozy room and sighed gustily. "Doesn't it do your heart good to be here?" he asked. "America's just going to soak this up. In this time of shaky values, the disintegration of the family, and Christmas so commercialized that ornaments hit the shelf in September, I bet we'll get a major share of the Christmas Eve audience."

It occurred to Jeff that Whittier was making every bit as commercial a venture of this Christmas as all the merchants he scorned, but it didn't seem politic to point it out.

Whittier looked across the table to Hartman. "We'll need you to pick us up about nine-thirty Christmas Eve to take us back to New York. Your agency said that'd be all right."

Hartman looked startled for a moment, then nodded. "Of course, Mr. Whittier."

"Wait." Jeff interceded on the driver's behalf. "He'll want to be with his family on Christmas Eve, Mr. Whittier."

Whittier raised an eyebrow. "So will I."

"Then maybe the agency can send someone else. Hartman's boys are coming home for Christmas for the first time in three years."

Whittier blinked at him, as though surprised he knew that. "I like Hartman. He drives me safely, but he gets me everywhere on time."

"I imagine Hartman's family likes him, too, and would want to be with him on Christmas Eve."

Whittier looked at Jeff as though he was beginning to wish him back in Lebanon.

"All right," he said finally. "I'll call this afternoon."

Jeff intercepted Hartman's grateful grin from across the table.

LIZA LED HER GUESTS on a quick tour of the house while Sherrie and Dora cleared away. Upstairs, she ushered her employer into a room Sherrie had decorated with her collection of quilts.

"Are these *the* quilts?" Whittier asked. "Edie told me that your column on making and collecting quilts got an enormous response."

"Yes, these are the ones I wrote about." Liza smiled as Whittier walked into the room and ran a hand over a colorful Ohio Star that Sherrie had draped over the footboard. It was nice to know, she thought, that that at least was the truth.

Liza pointed to the small door off his room. "That closet's been turned into a bathroom. It isn't very large, but if you don't mind having to shower rather than bathe, it has everything you need."

Whittier looked around with a satisfied nod. "Great," he said. "Well, if you don't mind, I'll freshen up, make a few phone calls, maybe rest an hour or so. Then Jeff and I can talk about what to discuss in his interview."

Liza turned to Jeff.

"Works for me," he said. He went back into the hall where Bill had left their bags lined up against the wall and, picking up the two largest ones, deposited them inside Whittier's door. "There you go. See you in a couple of hours."

"Thank you, Jeff." And Whittier closed the door on them.

Liza led Jeff to the next room, which had been decorated in light blue and white. Sherrie had added a red-and-white checked bedspread and a few primitive wooden art touches—a tall colonial soldier in a corner, a small military drum on the dresser and a pine wreath stuck with little American flags on the old oak armoire door.

Again she pointed to what had once been a closet. "Same bathroom setup as Mr. Whittier's. Towels and soap under the sink."

Liza watched him walk around the foot of the bed, put down a small brown bag and go to the window. She stayed in the doorway, but let herself study the back of him as he looked out onto the wintry landscape.

He wore black slacks and a simple black round-neck sweater that she guessed were brand-new. Of course, she thought. Escaping from captivity usually didn't allow for packing. For that matter, neither did being *taken* into captivity. She remembered hearing on the news that a French men's clothing manufacturer had given him a wardrobe in gratitude for his rescue of their countryman. She looked at the small brown bag and wondered where the rest of it was.

His shoulders were broad under the sweater, his waist slender, his hips lean, but muscled and taut under the stylish cut of the slacks.

His rich brown hair had been cut since she'd seen him on television, and he was now clean-shaven.

"This is so much more beautiful than sand," he said, then turned away from the window to smile at her. "It must be wonderful to live here."

His clear blue eyes met hers and for an instant she couldn't respond. She was going to have to lie, and that was a rotten thing to do to a man who'd just escaped hostile hands, saved the life of a priest, and who'd prevented her from breaking her neck when she fell off the ladder.

But she had to answer. *You do live here sometimes,* she rationalized. *When you visit Sherrie and the boys, you're not dead, are you? No. You're* living *here.*

Okay. It was a little thin, but still true.

"I do love it here," she agreed, evading his gaze by taking a few steps into the room and straightening the drum on the dresser.

When she looked up at him again, he was watching her, his eyes quiet but apparently interested in the nervous movement of her fingers atop the dresser. Pretending there was a purpose to her fiddling, she opened several drawers to show him they were empty.

"Lots of room for your things," she said, then pointed to his small suitcase. "Though you don't seem to have brought much. Didn't like the French designer's clothes?"

He laughed lightly. "I did. He gave me these, in fact." He plucked at the sleeve of his sweater. "I'm just generally not much of a fashion plate. I'm used to denim and cotton. I have a few other sweaters in the bag, and I brought along some old clothes I used to wear skiing so I can explore the countryside.''

Liza liked his lack of pretension. In fact, she was thinking that she liked a lot of things about him, and found herself wanting to do something she seldom felt inclined to do—flirt.

But he thought she was married.

There was little comfort to be found in the knowledge that she'd put *herself* in this position.

''I...I'm flattered,'' she said, maintaining her position near the dresser, ''that it was my fa—'' She stopped abruptly, smiled to distract him from her near gaffe, then added creatively, ''My apricot-glazed ham that inspired you to make it home. I've put it on the Christmas dinner menu.''

The tension in the room was palpable. *Oh, God,* she thought. *He knows I almost said that my face had drawn him home. He thinks I'm married, and that I'm hitting on him!*

A current of energy crackled between them, and though she clung to the corner of the dresser, she felt it trying to pull her toward him, drawing him toward her.

But he took a step backward and leaned a hip on the windowsill. ''Actually, Sylvia was watching you, and I passed through the room and thought how delicious the ham looked compared to the healthy pasta I'd just had.''

''Sylvia?''

''My fiancée.''

''Ah.''

Okay. Well. Just because he fits the role of Prince

Perfect in your fantasies, she told herself sharply, *doesn't mean he hasn't fulfilled his own fantasies long ago. The fact that you've been waiting for him for a lifetime doesn't mean he's been waiting for you. Damn it.*

She sighed theatrically, closing herself off and drawing in the little robot arm of sensors with which every single woman was equipped to analyze the single male for suitability as a mate.

"You're telling me that you don't really love my cooking, but that it was just preferable to the dull meal you'd just had?" She pretended injured feelings. Actually, her feelings *were* injured, but not because he preferred ham to pasta.

He grinned. "Don't tell your boss, or we'll be out on our collective ear, looking for a Christmas meal."

She forced herself to return his grin, thinking it sad that they didn't really have a collective ear. Or a collective anything.

"Your secret's safe with me," she said, going to the door. "Rest well."

He nodded. "Thank you."

Liza went to Bill's room, where he'd installed her the night before in the big oak four-poster. He had slept in the dressing room on a small sofa that opened into a single bed.

She went to the window and looked down at the same view Jeff saw from his window. The hills rolled away from the house toward distant mountains, a picturesque dotting of bare, lacy oaks against the heavy gunmetal gray of the sky. She wondered wryly if Ben Whittier had arranged to make it snow for Christmas.

Jeff James was engaged. She absorbed that fact
with a resentment she was disappointed to find in herself but indulged anyway. She would have to stop
thinking about him and concentrate on the special. He
belonged to someone else, but fifty-five minutes of
prime time belonged to her, and she had to pull it off
for the sake of her own career, for Edie's, and to get
the inn for Sherrie.

It was the mature thing to do.

Maturity, she thought, studying the stark landscape,
certainly bit the big one.

"How's it going?"

Liza turned from the window as Bill came into the
room, closing the door quietly behind him. He looked
concerned. "Something happen?"

"No," she assured him. "Everything's fine." She
made a self-deprecating face. "Thanks for saving me
with Betsy. I don't know why she hates me."

Bill smiled. "She doesn't hate you. But you're
tense every time you pick her up and she feels it, so
she screams."

"The boys never reacted to me that way."

"Everybody's different. Even at one year old. I put
her down in Sherrie's room, but I should probably
bring her crib in here. It'll look more natural if anybody wanders by."

Liza leaned a shoulder against one of the foot posts.
"Have I told you how much I appreciate your doing
this?"

"Several times," he said, going to the closet for a
blue-and-black buffalo plaid jacket. "But my motives
are purely selfish. If seeing me go to bed several

nights in a row with another woman doesn't shake Sherrie loose from her position on marriage, I give up.''

Liza shook her head. ''But she knows it's all an act, and that I'd never...''

''Well, don't let her know that you'd *never*,'' he warned, a devilish glint in his eye. ''If I'm right and she really does want me, she's too possessive a woman not to let jealousy take over.''

''How do you know that?''

''I've seen her with her children. A protective mother is usually a possessive wife.''

''But she's not your wife.''

''Are you paying attention?'' he asked with feigned impatience, pulling the jacket on. ''That's why we're here. I'm going out to get more firewood. See you later.''

Liza wanted to correct him and explain that *she* was here because she wanted to get to know Jeff James. But Bill was already out the door and Jeff James had a fiancée, anyway.

So she was here strictly to do a television show. A national television show.

She'd noticed earlier that Sherrie had planned a menu for the next few days as well as for the show, and listed for tonight was something called *Mandelbrot*.

Since Liza had no idea what it was, much less what was in it, she squared her shoulders and headed downstairs to investigate.

Chapter Four

Bill's kitchen smelled like a fine restaurant. The table in the dining room had been laid with a red-and-green-plaid tablecloth shot with gold thread, and a set of white, gold-rimmed china dinner plates stood in a stack on one end of the table. Beside it was a spray of tableware. A white poinsettia in a clay pot stood in the middle of the cloth.

Liza went through into the kitchen and found Sherrie and Dora hard at work. Dora was putting a roast into the oven while Sherrie peeled and chopped vegetables. Bing Crosby crooned Christmas carols from the CD player.

Liza felt as though she'd walked onto the set of *Holiday Inn.*

"Roast and vegetables," Liza said, watching Dora close the oven door on the large pan. "So *Mandelbrot*'s the bread?" she guessed, trying to think back to her one year of German in college. "*Brot?* Bread?"

Sherrie dropped a handful of chopped potatoes into a large bowl of water. "You're right about the bread part, but it's for dessert. Sort of like a biscotti. You've asked me to serve it with pudding, Miss De Lane.'' She took on a subservient tone of voice. ''Or should we call you Mrs. McBride?''

Liza came to stand beside her and look into her face, searching for signs of antagonism. But Sherrie smiled. It wasn't genuine, but it seemed intended to dismiss her concerns.

''How's Betsy?'' Sherrie asked, working a peeler expertly over a fat little carrot.

''Bill got her to sleep. He said we'd have to move her into our room on the chance that Whittier or Jeff walks by.''

Sherrie's hand froze for an instant over the word *our*, then continued to peel. Liza stored that information to tell Bill.

''You'd better give me something to do,'' Liza said, ''in case one of them comes down.''

''You could set the table.''

''I will. But besides that. I have to look like I know what I'm doing.''

Sherrie and Dora exchanged an amused look.

Liza put her hands on her hips, laughing. ''Look, I came down here to help, not to be insulted.''

''You helped make the hamburgers,'' Dora reminded her, giggling all the while, ''when Mr. McBride invited you all for the Fourth of July.''

''I remember.''

''We sliced them very thin and sold them to the high school's art class for charcoal.''

Liza threatened her with a look. "Ha, ha. Not funny. There must be something I can't screw up."

Sherrie handed her a divided bowl. "There are olives and peppers and pickles and that kind of stuff in the fridge. You could put them in here."

"Okay. I can handle that." Liza went to the refrigerator and carried bottles back to a corner of the counter.

Bill walked into the kitchen with an armload of wood and dropped it into the brass wood bin. Then he pulled off his jacket and poked at the dying fire with the end of a log.

"Hey, wife," he said with a wink in Liza's direction, "what are the chances of getting a cup of coffee?"

Liza glanced at Sherrie's back, but couldn't assess her reaction to the playful taunt.

"I'll get it for you, Mr. McBride." Dora made a face at him and went to pour him a mug.

Bill rolled his eyes at Liza, silently bemoaning his botched attempt to annoy Sherrie.

Liza had five of the six partitions in the condiment bowl filled when Sherrie tensed and stopped her work to listen. Bill had gone into his office with his coffee, and Dora was ironing linens in the laundry room.

"Was that Betsy?" she asked Liza.

Liza, too, stood quietly to listen but heard nothing. "I don't think so. The boys are playing in the back. It must have been them you heard."

Sherrie went back to work.

A few moments later footsteps sounded on the

stairs and Jeff appeared in the kitchen with Betsy riding his arm and clinging to his neck, her curly blond head resting on his shoulder.

"Look who's awake," he said.

"I thought I heard her," Sherrie said, moving as though to take the baby from him. Then, remembering her role, she remained with her vegetables and simply blew Betsy a kiss. "Hi, baby," she said.

Bracing herself, Liza went to take her.

Betsy started screaming the moment she approached. Determined not to let the baby ruin the scenario she'd created, Liza took her anyway and began bouncing her. She took her to the condiment bowl to try to distract her with the colors and shapes, to no avail.

Liza tossed her in the air and she screamed harder. Then she remembered the baby bottle of apple juice Sherrie had put in the refrigerator earlier that morning.

It plugged the noisy cavern for a moment, but just when Liza was about to congratulate herself on having saved the moment, Betsy threw the plastic bottle at her nose.

What must Jeff think, Liza wondered, frustrated and in pain, of a woman who couldn't appease her own baby?

Jeff took a banana from the fruit bowl on a corner of the counter, then came to Liza. Betsy reached out for it greedily.

"I think she blames me," Liza joked weakly, "for all those months of colic."

He laughed lightly, handing Betsy the banana. "One of my friend Abdul's twins was just like this. She just preferred men to women. Me, particularly."

Liza found that easy to believe.

Betsy shook the banana. When no rattling sound resulted, she explored it with baby fingertips, concentrating on the knobby black top.

The room was wonderfully quiet, except for Sherrie's chopping.

Jeff went to look over her shoulder. "Roast and vegetables?" he asked.

"Yes," she replied, handing him a carrot stick. "Liza thought you'd like real heart-of-America cooking tonight."

He smiled at Liza. "Thank you. Nothing in the world smells quite as good as that. But why aren't *you* cooking?"

It happened again. Liza opened her mouth to give him the excuse she and Sherrie had agreed upon, but no sound would come out. It was so hard to look into those wonderful blue eyes and lie.

"I volunteered," Sherrie finally said, "so she could have more time with her guests. She makes it look easy, but there's a lot of preparation time in some things, and...you weren't invited here to sit around and watch her chop vegetables and knead bread."

Liza breathed a sigh of relief and shot Sherrie a grateful look.

JEFF DIDN'T KNOW if it was the months of foreign cuisine followed by ten weeks of nothing but rice and other things he never analyzed too closely, but he'd never tasted anything quite as wonderful as Sherrie's roast and potatoes.

He and Bill and the boys were left at the table over second helpings while Sherrie and Liza went into the kitchen to get dessert. Dora had left on her night off, and Whittier had excused himself to make a phone call.

"More wine?" Bill asked.

"Please." Jeff watched him top up his wineglass and still manage to quell his boys, growing rambunctious after the long meal, with a glance down the table.

"Dessert looks really good," he said amiably. "You don't want to risk missing it. Either finish up, or carry your plates into the kitchen."

The boys picked up their plates and bolted for the swinging door, energy exuding from them even at seven o'clock at night.

"Nice boys," Jeff said, thinking it strange that he wanted to resent this man because he had precisely what he wanted—or *who* he wanted—but he was so amiable that it was impossible.

Bill smiled and leaned back in his chair with his glass. "Thank you. Their mother's mostly responsible. I leave them alone a lot."

"You travel in your work?"

"Only between here and the hospital. I've been a pediatrician there for eight years. Fortunately, my partners are working through the holiday so…so I can be in Liza's show."

"Is it hard to have a celebrity wife?"

He thought about it a moment. "No. I get to be her tasting panel, so that's pretty great." He looked around him. "And it's hard to complain about her absorption in her crafts when the house ends up looking like this."

"True." It was warm and elegant and made you feel as though you'd died and gone to mother-love heaven.

"You've never been married?" Bill asked.

Jeff shook his head. "I traveled around a lot as a kid, working all over the world. Then I came home for a while, started my own engineering firm, fell in love...." He swept the air with a hand, trying to express the unexplainable fact of love that didn't last. "When it all fell apart, I took the job in Beirut. You know the rest of the story."

"You'll find love again," Bill assured him. "With your face all over the news, you'll probably look up after the first of the year to find a thousand women on your doorstep and more book and endorsement offers than you can handle."

But not the *right* woman.

"I understand Sherrie cooked the roast," Jeff said conversationally, hoping to change the subject.

Bill looked at him for a minute and Jeff could have sworn he saw antagonism in his face and a flicker of temper. In the moment it took him to recognize and wonder at that instant change in mood, it was gone.

"Sherrie's practically engaged," Bill said, downing the rest of his wine. "To some bodybuilder in New Haven. His father was in the Mafia, I heard."

And while Jeff struggled with the image of a Mafia muscleman taking the graceful and competent Sherrie for a wife, dessert arrived, and Whittier returned to the table.

Travis took a bite of the cookie served on the saucer under a goblet of pudding. "Yum, Mom," he said to Liza. "The cookies are great."

"They're called *Mandelbrot*, sweetie," she said. "Almond bread. They're often prepared for Hanukkah."

"That's the Jewish Christmas," Davey told Jeff.

Jeff nodded, finishing a bite of cookie. He swallowed. "Right. These cookies make you wish it was Hanukkah all year round, don't they?"

"Yeah. We're gonna get bikes for Christmas!" the boy announced, his face aglow.

His brother elbowed him fiercely, and there was sudden tension around the table. Davey rubbed his arm, looking stricken. Somebody, Jeff guessed, had found the stash of presents—although he couldn't imagine there was more than the treasure trove already under the tree.

"How do you know you're getting bikes?" Whittier asked, leaning toward Davey. "Santa doesn't come until the day after tomorrow."

"Well…" Davey turned to his mother.

"Davey's an optimist," Liza said, reaching out to touch his cheek affectionately. "He asked for a bike, so he feels pretty sure he's going to get one."

"But he won't," Travis put in, making a face at his brother, "because he hasn't been *good.*"

"I have too!" Davey insisted, half out of his chair.

"Have not."

"Have *too!*"

Liza pushed Davey back into his chair and Bill turned that silencing look on Travis, who dipped his spoon into his pudding.

Liza looked across the table at Jeff. "See what you're missing by being single? You, too, could have squabbles at the dinner table every night."

"I just told him," Bill said, "that every woman in the country's going to be after him as soon as the holidays are over."

"My secretary just told me that Larry King and 'Sixty Minutes' called." Whittier added cream to his coffee, then looked up at Jeff. "You're going to have to start thinking about an agent or a business manager."

Jeff shook his head. "I don't think so. I don't like other people in control of my life."

"That's what happens when you get married," Bill observed mildly.

Liza socked him in the arm. He winced theatrically, and the boys laughed.

"But you'll want to take advantage of your moment in the spotlight," Whittier insisted. "Fame is fleeting, remember. This is a window of opportunity, but a small one."

"I don't want to romanticize what happened," Jeff said. Even now, in a private moment, he could draw into himself and remember the physical and emotional misery of his captivity, the indomitable courage of Father Chabot, and the absolute, though mad, sincerity of his captors. "I couldn't capitalize on my experience."

Bill met his gaze. "The world needs heroes, Jeff. Your story would give boys like Travis and Davey someone to believe in besides spoiled athletes and bored and reckless movie stars."

"Then you should talk to Father Chabot. I had the courage to keep going once I was out of there. But he had the courage to go from day to day when it looked as though nothing would ever change, as though we'd be there forever. And he'd been in a few months longer than I had."

"Jeff." Whittier put a hand on his arm, apparently to claim his full attention. "I'm talking about big money. *Big* money."

Jeff understood him completely. Big money was the man's job, his purpose in life. And while Jeff could appreciate financial gain as a goal, it had never really been his objective.

He appreciated the comfortable life a reasonable income gave him, but he thrived on the bigness of a project, the distant spaces it brought together—both sides of a river, two sides of a city that couldn't be connected through it because of a warren of dusty little streets and narrow alleyways. He got a thrill out of bringing water to thirsty people.

So he built bridges and freeways and water systems. And there had been times, he thought whimsically, remembering a thirsty little village in Chad, when the people's gratitude had made him feel like Santa Claus.

"I'd rather hold out," he said, "for a big job. I've hardly been able to move for the last three months, and now that I'm free, I have serious cabin fever. So I'm going to travel for a few weeks thanks to a bank account I left in Boston, then find work."

"But you accepted my invitation to do this show."

Jeff was careful not to look in Liza's direction, afraid someone would read in his eyes why he'd done it.

"As I recall, I accepted an invitation to spend Christmas with Liza De Lane. It was only after I accepted that you told me there was a television show involved."

Whittier was incredulous. "What'll I tell Larry King and 'Sixty Minutes'?"

"Tell them to call Father Chabot," he replied. "The doctor said he's going to be fine. And I'm sure he'd like to make big bucks for his community of priests and their work with the poor."

Whittier apparently chose to try one more time. "Jeff. You have to think of this from a reporter's point of view—from the perspective of an audience hungry for information. *You* carried Father Chabot to safety, you kept him alive for six days when he'd been shot, you stole food and fed him before you ate."

Jeff nodded, also choosing to try one more time. "What you're not getting, Mr. Whittier, is that…he's the one who got me to the point where I could do that. He taught me to pray and to believe when there was nothing to hold on to. *He's* the hero.''

Jeff looked into Whittier's eyes, hoping for understanding, but saw only the same mystified expression he'd worn before. This, Jeff accepted, was a distance he couldn't bridge with steel and good engineering.

''But we don't have to worry about that for a couple of days, do we?'' he asked.

''That's right,'' Bill said. ''You're here to enjoy Christmas with us, so let's not worry about the past or the future. This moment is too important.''

As everyone stood and Jeff helped the boys collect dishes, he caught the exchange of a glance between Sherrie and Bill. It was difficult to define, and it was over in an instant, but for Jeff it caused a small disturbing ripple on the surface of the evening.

They moved to the living room and watched several Christmas specials, which Whittier critiqued and made notes on while Liza and Sherrie stuffed everyone with samples of more holiday treats.

When everyone pleaded for mercy, Liza sat on the sofa beside Bill, his arm casually around her, and the children sprawled around them, Davey falling asleep with his head in Liza's lap.

Sherrie sat apart from everyone in a chair near the fire, looking through a cookbook and taking notes.

Jeff, in the other chair, leaned toward her and asked quietly, ''Are you getting background for the show?''

She looked up at him, her expression disgruntled, then she smiled, as though she'd had to force it. ''Yes.

I'm looking up the history of *Mandelbrot* for Liza, since everyone seemed to enjoy it so much. She'll...probably want to include it in the show.''

"Do you help with the column, too?"

"No!" Her reply was quick and emphatic, then she smiled again and closed the book. "No. I helped her with a small cable show last year, but this year...I mean, this one's national and I'm doing most of her research, so I'm a little...edgy."

She was. He'd noticed that she'd grown more quiet and more remote as the evening wore on. Except for that look she'd exchanged with Bill.

Jeff refused to even consider what that could mean. And it wasn't his business, anyway.

"I'm nervous, too," he said conversationally. "It's my first time on television—cable or national." Then he remembered a bridge he'd worked on in Malaysia. "No, I take that back. There was one time when the local TV station came out for the ribbon-cutting of a bridge I worked on in Sarawak. I was on the evening news in a hard hat and a poncho because it was pouring. You couldn't even tell it was me. Talk about a small window of opportunity."

She laughed and put the book aside, the disgruntled look fading. "I admire your unwillingness to make money your bottom line. I'd like to be that noble."

He shrugged a shoulder. "I have only myself to support. What do you do when you're not helping your sister with a television show?"

"I'm the chef at the Rockbury Inn in town."

"Do you have a family? Bill told me you're dating someone."

She looked distracted for a moment. "Sort of," she said.

When he raised an eyebrow at that, she laughed again. "Um...I mean that I...borrow Liza's family a lot. And the man I'm—er—seeing...it's not serious. Actually, I'm waiting for Tom Selleck."

"Ah." He laughed. "He's getting a little mature for you, isn't he?"

She grinned wickedly. "That's what I like about him. I married youth and charm once. This time I *want* maturity. And the fact that he's gorgeous—with or without the mustache—doesn't hurt."

"Isn't he married to a dancer?"

She waved a hand airily. "Oh, he'll get tired of beauty and a tight little body. When he comes looking for the best pot roast he's ever had, I'll be here."

"Good plan."

She grew serious suddenly. "What are you looking for?"

He didn't have to think about that. She was sitting on the sofa in another man's arms. But from a guest in her home, that would be a poor answer. He pretended to consider.

"A cheerful nature," he replied finally. "Someone willing to travel with me. To have children."

She frowned. "Travel and children don't go together very well. Children need a predictable routine."

"Couldn't they have a predictable routine in a foreign place?"

"I don't know. My..." She stopped and cleared her throat. "My nephews...were very upset with the move."

"What move?"

"Ah...here. To Rockbury. They hated leaving their schools."

"So the boys aren't Bill's?" he asked.

She looked startled. "Why?"

"Because he told me he's been at Rockbury Hospital for eight years. Travis would have been two and not in school, and Davey wasn't even born yet."

"No." Her eyes went across the room to where Liza and Bill and the boys sat together, to Whittier in the recliner, toward the kitchen, then back to him. "They summered here when they were first married, then decided to move here, but it...it took a while. Bill commuted."

"Until after the boys started school? That must have been an ordeal."

"It was only from Hartford." She stood abruptly, her hands moving nervously up and down her arms. "If you'll excuse me, I have some things to get ready for tomorrow. Can I bring you a brandy before bed, or anything?"

"No, thanks." He stood also. "I think I'll head up now."

"See you in the morning."

Jeff turned to say good-night to his hosts and encountered Bill's distrustful gaze. Liza was talking to

Travis, who leaned sleepily against her, and Whittier remained glued to the television.

Jeff refocused on Bill's face, trying to analyze what it meant. He didn't like the only answer he could think of to explain the man's behavior.

Both times Jeff had met that look he'd been talking to Sherrie. And he recalled the glance Bill and Sherrie had exchanged when everyone else had been clearing the table. It hadn't been loving, but it had had an edge of urgency that developed between people who cared deeply for each other.

He didn't even want to form the thought into words, but his brain did it anyway. Did Liza's husband and her sister have something going?

Bill's expression changed to one of hospitable amiability. "You going up, Jeff?"

"Yes," he said, trying, as Bill apparently was, to pretend they hadn't just looked daggers at each other. "Thank you again for a wonderful dinner and for your hospitality. I'm usually an early riser, so if you wake up and find me gone, don't worry."

"We're planning breakfast for eight," Liza said, looking up from her son. She looked flushed and sleepy and he had to force himself not to stare. "But if you're having a good time exploring, we'll leave your plate in the oven."

"Thank you."

As Jeff turned to the stairs, Bill said to Liza, "Why don't you go up with him, sweetheart, and make sure he has enough towels, and can find extra blankets."

Liza met Jeff's eyes, then turned to Travis, who'd

fallen asleep against her shoulder. "You do it, Bill," she argued gently. "I have to get the boys to bed."

"I'll do that in a minute," he insisted. "You see Jeff upstairs."

It was clear that she didn't want to. Jeff couldn't believe Bill couldn't see that. It was possible he was encouraging her so that he could have a private moment in the kitchen with Sherrie.

Jeff realized that was all conjecture on his part, and he pushed the thought away so that Liza couldn't read it in him. She had a way of looking into his eyes that told him she read his mind and, what was worse, his heart.

Bill reached around her to support Travis so that Liza could stand, then he pulled the boy toward him and he was asleep again before his head hit Bill's shoulder.

Jeff waited at the bottom of the stairs and stood aside to let Liza go up ahead of him. He kept a safe distance behind her, then followed her into the room.

She flipped on the light and went to the armoire, pulling open the bottom drawer.

He let his eyes slip over her delicious curves, then wiped the desire from his face when she straightened with a plaid wool blanket in her arms.

"They're promising snow for tomorrow," she said, kicking the drawer closed with her foot, "so it'll be cold tonight. This should be enough with the comforter."

He agreed with a nod and watched her shake the blanket out atop his bed. "I'd put it under your comforter," she said without looking at him, "but it's pretty prickly. It'll still keep you warm this way."

She would keep him warmer, he thought, but that was out of the question.

Her task completed, she took a step toward him, expecting, he supposed, that he would move out of her way. But he didn't. He couldn't have her for a lifetime, but he was damn well going to enjoy looking at her for the few minutes allowed him.

"I'm very grateful you invited me," he said, holding his position. "I'm so glad to be back in the States, but I hadn't really felt as though I'd come home until I walked into your house."

Her eyes widened and softened, and he thought for a moment she might come toward him. But she took hold of the foot post on the bed and held tightly.

"We're happy to have you," she said in a quiet voice. "Despite all your denials, you're a hero and we're...we're honored that you agreed to be our guest."

He grinned at her. "Whittier bullied you into inviting me, didn't he?"

"No. He didn't." Her denial was quiet but emphatic. "I...we...wanted to meet you."

He read between the words. *I...we.* She'd wanted to meet him, but she couldn't admit that. He wondered if she suspected that something was going on between her sister and her husband. Or if she knew for certain and considered planning her own diversion.

"I can't believe your fiancée let you come to Connecticut for Christmas," she said. "I'd have moved heaven and earth…"

There was that telltale pause again. *She* would have moved heaven and earth. Did she mean for Bill, or for him?

He decided to test the waters. He'd never try to lure a woman away from another man, but if she was being treated unfairly and wanted to leave, that was another story.

He leaned an elbow on the dresser. "Actually, Sylvia and I parted company just before I left for Lebanon. She's married someone else."

"Really?" He wasn't sure if she smiled or if he just *wanted* to see a smile on her face at that news and imagined it there. In any case, if it had been there, it hadn't lasted more than an instant. She now studied him soberly. "I'm sorry. That must have been very painful for you."

He made a so-so gesture with his hand. "I knew it had been falling apart, but I didn't understand why. So I didn't do anything about it." He looked into her eyes. "It's a policy with me not to act until I have all the facts in a situation."

She stared back at him. He knew she knew what he was telling her. But she dropped her hands from the post and took a step back. He understood that she was putting distance between them. So that was that.

"Good for you," she said with a wry smile. "I always jump in with both feet, fueled by perpetual enthusiasm and the unshakable belief that it'll all turn out well in the end.''

"How often have you been wrong?"

"So far I'm fifty-fifty." She came toward him. In truth, he knew her purpose was only to try to leave the room, and he stood in front of the only exit.

He didn't move. "I like better odds than that," he said.

This time she looked into his eyes—and held them. "That must be why you left a building filled with armed men, without a weapon of your own, half-carrying an old man."

Distracted by the indecipherable message in her dark eyes, he let her pass him.

"Good night, Jeff," she called from the hallway.

He stepped out in it as she turned at the head of the stairs and disappeared. He stood there in the dim light, remembering her velvet eyes boring into his with a message he couldn't quite interpret. She knew he took chances? She wanted him to take a chance on her? But she hadn't touched him, and certainly she would have if that had been her point.

Great. For a man who didn't make a move without full understanding of all the details, this was not a good position.

Unless he changed his style.

Chapter Five

Liza sat in the middle of the stairs, trembling with frustration and exasperation. Her elbows resting on her knees, her face buried in her hands, she remembered Jeff's strong, supple body blocking her exit from his bedroom.

He knew she was interested in him. And she was sure he was interested in her. If this situation wasn't handled carefully, it could explode in so many directions that the air she breathed would be poisoned for generations.

She couldn't tell him she wasn't married, but if she failed to make it clear to him that they could have a relationship when this show was over, he could be off on his two-week odyssey, take a job halfway across the world and she'd never see him again.

So she had to somehow hold his interest without looking like a bored matron prowling for an affair.

Right now she had no idea how she could do that. Not with Whittier dogging their every step.

Liza made her way to the kitchen, mentally and physically exhausted. But Sherrie had been working like a slave all day, and she was going to clean up for her so she could go to bed.

Unfortunately, Bill and Whittier sat at the table sipping brandies while Sherrie whipped up something in a bowl.

"But while you were putting the boys to bed," Whittier was saying to Bill, "Sherrie told me that you and Liza met at a church dance in Hartford."

Sherrie's whisk paused in its frantic movements, then picked up speed again and continued.

Liza caught Bill's eye worriedly over Whittier's head.

"We did," Bill insisted, taking another sip.

Whittier folded his arms on the table. "But you just said it was a blind date."

"It was a blind date at a church dance," Liza said after a moment's consideration. It seemed almost too simple a solution to the trip-up in stories. Hoping to appear casual, she opened the dishwasher, but found that Sherrie had already emptied it. Liza closed it again. "His friend was dating Sherrie, and she brought me for Bill."

She took the jug of milk off the counter and carried it to the refrigerator, waiting for the story to explode on her. But it didn't.

Whittier accepted that explanation with a roll of his eyes. "My blind dates never turned out looking like Liza. My friends fixed me up with women who looked like longshoremen or prison matrons. Well..." He tipped his balloon glass back, downed the last drop of brandy and got to his feet.

"Thank you all for a delightful evening. What time's breakfast?"

Sherrie was still whipping madly.

"Eight o'clock," Liza replied.

"Great. I'll be down for it. I presume since Sherrie's whipping up batter, we're going to be treated to your famous flapjacks?"

Right. Her famous flapjacks. She'd mentioned several times in her column how she flipped them for her children and caught them in the pan. "But of course."

"And you'll wait until I get down to flip one?"

Oh, God. "You bet."

Whittier reached out impulsively to hug her. "Thank you, Liza," he said, his cheeks glowing, his eyes dancing merrily. She suspected it was from too much brandy, rather than the result of the spirit of the season. "Thank you for making these few days possible."

The moment his footsteps topped the stairs and sounded in the hallway overhead, Sherrie turned from the flapjack batter and wiped her hands on her apron. Her glance was deadly. "Yes, Liza," she said. "Thank you for making these few days possible."

Liza guessed that was exhaustion talking. She went to put an arm around her. "I'm sorry. I know you've been worked to a nub, but when it's over you can buy the inn. Just keep thinking about that."

"Really?" Sherrie shook her arm off and covered the bowl of batter with plastic wrap. "Bill thinks I'd make a terrible proprietor."

Liza frowned at Bill.

"What I said was…" He eyed Sherrie in complete exasperation, an elbow braced on the back of his chair. "That if you're going to explode at every little suggestion made by—"

"He said it was embarrassing for everyone that I was *flirting* with Jeff!" Sherrie put the bowl in the refrigerator and gave the door a vicious swing closed. "I made mulled cider, gingerbread, pot roast and vegetables, pudding and *Mandelbrot!* When in the hell did I have time to flirt?"

"You worked it in smoothly while Liza and I were watching television," Bill replied, making no effort to defuse the situation.

Liza turned the frown to a glare. "Bill," she warned.

"Don't give me that look," he said. "It only works when you're really married."

"We were talking about what we wanted in mates," Sherrie said with an air of wounded dignity. "That was all. I was fishing because Liza likes him."

Bill looked at Liza in surprise. "You do?"

She nodded. "But thanks to the surprisingly smooth workings of my plan, he believes I'm married and so I can't really…act interested."

The three of them stared gloomily at each other.

Liza pushed Sherrie toward the stairs. "You go to bed and I'll finish cleaning up. I'll even set the table for breakfast."

Sherrie sighed. "All right." She pulled the apron off and hung it on a hook in the utility closet. "Oh, incidentally," she said, "if Jeff should mention it, I told him you lived here summers, then when Bill got the job at the hospital, he commuted between here and Hartford until after the boys started school.''

"Why," he implored, "did you say that?"

She turned on him angrily. "Because it's hard to keep it all straight, all right? Because he was talking about wanting a woman who'd be willing to move around the world with him on engineering projects but still want to have children, and I said that children needed routine, and I happened to mention that Travis and Davey had been shaken by the move here." She drew a breath and glowered at Bill. "But you had already told him that you'd been with the hospital for eight years, so he couldn't imagine how the boys could be traumatized when Travis would have been only two and not even in school, and Davey wasn't even born yet. So I had to improvise. I know it wasn't great, but I'm sorry. I never claimed to be Mata Hari.''

Liza took hold of Sherrie's shoulders and gave her a small shake. "Sherrie, I'm sorry to be putting you through this, really I am. But you're doing great. It'll all come together, I promise.''

"Yeah," she said, heading for the stairs. "But it seems to be causing other things to fall apart.''

Liza sat at the table, leaving a chair between her and Bill. They heard the sound of Sherrie's bedroom door closing upstairs.

"Do you think she meant the two of you are falling apart?'' Liza asked.

Bill shrugged a shoulder moodily. "Possibly. But

the point she isn't getting is that if she won't commit to us, there's nothing there to fall apart in the first place."

"Come on, Bill," she cajoled. "You're not being very compassionate. She's confused."

Bill met her gaze, and for the first time since Sherrie had introduced her to him more than a year ago, she saw the frustrated man under the usually mellow doctor.

"So am I," he replied. "And being compassionate has gotten me nowhere."

"Just last night," she reminded him gently, "you were looking forward to using this as an opportunity to make her realize that she does love and need you. Forgive me, but your approach needs some refinement."

He groaned and ran a hand over his face. "I hadn't counted on it being this difficult to have her around all the time and not be able to touch her. To know that she's just down the hall and not be able to do anything about it. To have her look daggers at me because our little arrangement requires me to be attentive to you."

"Whittier leaves right after the show on Christmas Eve," Liza said. "I am willing to bet you that you'll get just what you want for Christmas—my sister."

He studied her with an even glance, then asked quietly, "Have you thought about how many of us you'll have to answer to if this all goes bad on us before the show?"

She sighed, suddenly more weary than she could

bear. "It's all I think about. But everyone has too much at stake. I won't let it go bad. Trust me, Bill."

He stared at her another moment, then pushed away from the table and got to his feet. "I will, Liza," he said. "I just hope to hell you know what you're talking about. I'll bring in another load of wood before I go upstairs. Anything I can do for you?"

She looked around the almost spotless kitchen. "Thanks, but it'll only take me a few minutes. Sherrie tidies up as she works. A good quality in a woman."

He grinned at her over his shoulder as he headed for the door. "Save your breath. I'm already sold."

LIZA AWOKE TO FUSSY CRIES and wondered drowsily how a cat had gotten into her high-rise apartment. Then the sound grew louder and she came awake with sudden urgency, realizing that the sound came from Betsy.

Bill, beyond the louvered doors, was fast asleep, and Sherrie was probably too exhausted for anything to penetrate her sleep.

Liza put on the bedside light and went to the baby, prepared for her to continue screaming even after she'd been picked up.

Betsy didn't disappoint her. Liza turned to the bed to change her, and in her bare feet stepped on something small and fuzzy. The discordant, manufactured squeak assured her that it wasn't a mouse, so she reached down to pick it up. It was Betsy's small stuffed bear.

Betsy grabbed it from her, cuddled it in her arm

and leaned heavily against Liza's shoulder. Liza stood still for a moment, stunned by that response. This was Betsy, who had hated her since birth.

She laid her down on the bed, certain she would protest noisily, but she simply cuddled her bear and watched Liza's face with sleepy interest until she'd finished diapering.

When Liza lifted her into her arms again, she snuggled close and was asleep in minutes. She was restored to the crib without waking.

Liza stood over her, recognizing the event for the momentous breakthrough that it was. Though it was only two in the morning, today was December 23— deep into the season of miracles.

She felt a sense of invincibility. She would pass off Bill and her nephews as her family for the sake of everyone involved, but the moment the show was over, she would take Jeff aside, explain the situation, ask him to forgive the deception and invite him out on a date.

Yes, it was simple and straightforward, but so was she—when she wasn't trying to deceive an entire country.

Feeling restless and energized by her decision, she pulled on the big blue robe Bill had left over the chair and went downstairs, intent on a cup of tea and possibly a piece of *Mandelbrot* the boys had missed.

She was surprised and a little dismayed to find Jeff, dressed in a pair of old gray woolen pants and a dark-blue-and-gray sweater with a blue turtleneck. He was staring out the kitchen window.

He turned when he heard her approach. He held a mug of coffee in his hand, and she noticed that the deep blue of the sweater close to his face darkened the color of his eyes. He looked very wide awake, and despite the fact that he seemed relaxed, she thought she sensed an alertness come over him, as though he couldn't be himself with her, as though her presence required caution.

She regretted that and wished desperately that she could explain. But she couldn't, and there was no point bemoaning the fact.

"Hi," she said, giving him only a friendly, casual glance as she went to the stove to get the kettle. "I'm sorry, did the baby wake you?"

"No. I've been down here for a while." He moved aside so that she could put the kettle under the faucet. "I heard her, though. Is everything all right?"

"Oh, yes." She carried the kettle to the stove, the tension she'd felt in his room last night snaking its way around her right now. "She just wakes up and wants to know somebody's there." At least, that was how Sherrie had explained it to her.

"I don't think that's something we ever outgrow." He leaned back against the counter and turned his head to watch her as she reached into an overhead cupboard for a cup. "My parents were older and I remember how quiet our house always was. I loved them, but I used to hate the quiet. I wanted the noise and excitement of my friends' houses, full of other kids and football games on TV and dogs barking."

Liza understood completely. That was the kind of

fictional world she'd built in her columns, a busy country home where something was always going on.

"Then I finished school and got busy," he continued, waving his mug to indicate, she guessed, the forward progression of his life. "I loved my work and I loved the travel, and decided that maybe I didn't need those things after all."

"But you had a fiancée," Liza said over her shoulder as she pulled down a box of tea, unwrapped a bag and placed it in her cup.

He nodded. "Sylvia Stanford. We were perfect for each other...." He gave her a grinning glance. "Or so I thought, because she was as devoted to her work as I was to mine."

"What did she do?"

"She runs a test kitchen for Sunquick. You know, the foods conglomerate?"

"No kidding!" The real Liza used their canned and microwavable products all the time. "I love that stuff." When he looked surprised, she added quickly and, she thought, cleverly, "When the boys have games or I'm otherwise pressed for time, they're a great fill-in for meals."

"Ah." He seemed to accept that as logical. "Anyway, she put in long hours, often worked on recipes at home. I thought what we had was perfect because she didn't resent it when I had to be away, and it didn't bother me that she often worked late. I thought it was love because we didn't distract each other."

Liza found the plate of *Mandelbrot*. Two lone

pieces were covered in plastic wrap. She pulled the wrap off and offered him a cookie.

"Is it all right for us to take the last two?" he asked.

She smiled. "It's all right for me. I'm going to blame you."

He took a cookie. "In that case, I may as well be guilty."

The kettle began to boil and Liza hurried to it before it could whistle in the quiet house. She poured water into her cup, then waved Jeff to follow her.

She went to a window seat in a far corner of the kitchen. The cushions on it had been covered with a red-and-beige check to match the curtains at the window.

She sat in one corner of the seat and held one side of the curtains back to look outside. She gasped in pleased surprise at the sight of large snowflakes drifting from the sky.

"It's snowing!" she exclaimed in a loud whisper as Jeff settled in the other corner of the seat.

He smiled at her excitement. "I thought you knew. It's beautiful, isn't it? It seems a miracle of nature that something can so change the look of the world without making a sound."

"I love snow out here," she said, her guard slipping a little in their comfortable midnight conversation. "It looks so different in New York."

As soon as the words were out of her mouth, she panicked. Then she realized that to him, it had probably been a perfectly reasonable thing to say. He didn't know she was thinking of how it looked from her high-rise window.

"Do you have to spend much time there?" he asked.

"Not much." She took a deep sip of tea, then brought him back to their interrupted discussion about Sylvia. "I take it your relationship with Sylvia turned out...not to be love after all?"

"No, it wasn't. I thought we had a good thing going because we didn't distract each other. Then it turned out that she'd been spending some of those late nights with a Dallas rancher doing banking business in Boston, and she left to marry him." He dunked his cookie in the tea, then rested it on his cup as he apparently thought over the past. "Then it occurred to me that it couldn't have been love, because love *has* to distract you. It should slow you down, reel you in, make you look at your world and what's in it and face it honestly. Like Christmas does." He bit into the cookie.

Liza looked out at the snow and wondered what he would think if he slowed down and looked around and learned that she wasn't married at all. Her confidence of a few moments ago in the ultimate result of this Christmas "play" deflated a little at his analysis of how love should behave. Was it possible to face a dishonest situation in an honest way?

"Does your marriage do that for you?" he asked, startling her out of her thoughts.

"What?"

"Does your marriage ground you? Your celebrity

must be unsettling sometimes. Bill seems very...
solid.''

Liza couldn't quite define her suspicion, but she
thought there was a kind of test in the question. He'd
asked it casually, but she sensed a certain tension in
him as he waited for her answer. He might very well
have concluded that she was attracted to him and put
that down to an unhappy marriage.

But even though she wasn't married to Bill, the
man had turned his life upside down to help her and
he was the soul of kindness and consideration. She
couldn't let Jeff believe ill of him.

"Bill's a wonderful man," she said sincerely.
"He's as fine and caring in his relationships as he is
with his patients."

"So you're still very much in love after...what?
Twelve years of marriage?"

"Twelve years of marriage," she agreed, deliberately sidestepping the very-much-in-love part.

He studied her, as though gauging the truthfulness
of her reply. She did her best to return his gaze with
innocence in hers.

"Your sister tells me she's divorced," he said.

She frowned. All she needed to complicate the situation was to have him develop an interest in Sherrie!

"Yes," she answered. "Why?"

He shook his head. "No reason." He grinned.
"She said she was waiting for Tom Selleck to get
bored with his wife and come looking for a good pot
roast."

Liza laughed, then sipped her tea. "She's always

been a nut. I don't think she'd like Hollywood, though. She's too attached to Connecticut.''

Jeff held his side of the curtains back and watched the snow drift down onto the already blanketed countryside. "I could grow attached to it, too. They don't need bridges or freeways here, though. Too bad.''

"That isn't all engineers do, is it?''

"No. But it's what I like to do.''

"Oh.''

Liza let it rest, knowing any more protestation on her part wouldn't fit the role she'd assumed. She made a mental note to consult a psychiatrist the moment this was over.

"How long has Sherrie worked with you?'' Jeff asked.

That answer required care. And why did he insist on talking about Sherrie? "We were raised by a single mother who worked a lot, so we were always helping each other with things. She helped me do the cable show last Christmas, and I consult her once in a while when I'm developing a recipe.''

"She enjoys being with your family.''

"Well…she thinks of my kids as hers. And Bill does a lot of her handyman stuff.''

Jeff was quiet. Liza studied him, sensing something restrained in the silence.

Then she understood what it was. *She* was being restrained. What she wanted to do was grab him by the shoulders and ask him if she was correct in feeling that he was interested in her, if she was simply misinterpreting his looks in her direction, his curious questions, or if he was trying to find out if she cared about him.

Because if he was, she *wasn't married*.

But that was too dangerous. Right now, restraint had to be her byword.

She stood abruptly. "I'd better get back to bed. Are you going to be all right down here? Would you like me to build a fire?" She prayed he would refuse her. She hadn't built a fire since Girl Scouts, and then she'd ignited the troop leader's skirt.

"Thanks, but I'm going up, too." He stood also and took her cup. "Go ahead. I'll be right behind you."

"All right. Good night."

Liza hadn't realized he meant that quite so literally until she'd climbed several steps, her mind on the mysterious engineer instead of the long robe she wore, and tripped over it.

She fell forward and sideways with a little cry of alarm. She hit her knee on a stair and gritted her teeth against a sideways crash with the railing and probably a sideways bump from stair to stair all the way down to the carpet. But it didn't happen.

She collided, all right, but with the front of Jeff's sweater, not the railing. He'd stretched out his body from the step below hers and placed himself between her and the balusters.

Her chin smacked into his shoulder and for a moment the world reeled. When it was steady again, she realized that he had an arm under her head and that his free hand was inside the waist of her robe, unfastened in the fall.

"You came down hard on your ribs," he said. "Are you all right?"

It took her a moment to answer—not because her ribs hurt, but because she was just where she'd wanted to be from the moment she'd seen him on television.

"I think...so," she said breathlessly. His closeness trapped the air in her lungs. If she moved her head an inch in his direction, her cheek would touch his.

"Are you sure?" His thumb ran gently over the jut of her ribs. "Take a deep breath. If you've broken anything, it'll hurt like hell."

She didn't think she had a deep breath in her. Or if she did, her body wasn't bothering to use it. Her entire awareness was filled with the ironlike quality of the muscular arm under her head, the tenderness of the fingertips probing her ribs through the flannel pajamas, the long, strong leg braced over her on a stair to keep both of them from falling.

"I'm...okay," she insisted on a whisper.

"Well, sit up carefully."

She complied, his long body still cupping hers protectively. She would have given a year of her life, she thought, to be able to turn her face into his shoulder.

She'd have given her entire old age to have been able to wrap her arms around him and kiss his lips. Unless, of course, there was any chance she'd be able to spend her old age *with* him.

She drew a deep breath, more because she needed it than to judge the condition of her ribs.

He watched her diagnostically. "Okay?"

"Yes," she said. "Okay."

And then he did the unheard-of, only-in-romance-novels, fairy-tale thing. He lifted her into his arms and carried her the rest of the way up the stairs.

She was enjoying it with a blissfulness she was sure few women ever knew when it occurred to her that she was in serious trouble if he walked her into Bill's room and saw that Bill wasn't in her bed.

"I can walk," she said, pushing against his shoulder.

They passed Whittier's room, and Jeff kept walking.

She kicked her feet. "Jeff, I can..."

Then Providence intervened and Bill appeared in the doorway in the gray sweat suit he wore to bed. He looked rumpled and perplexed.

"There you are," he said to Liza, then looked from her to Jeff. "What happened?"

Jeff placed her in Bill's arms. "She fell on the stairs. She says she's all right, but you...might want to be sure. Good night."

"Good...night." Bill stared after him in wonder, then looked down at Liza in concern.

"Are you all right?"

"I'm fine," she insisted. "You can put me down."

"You're sure?"

"I'm sure."

"You're trembling."

"It's two-thirty on a December morning in Connecticut, Bill. It's cold. Will you please put me down?"

A door down the hall was yanked open and a disheveled blond head peered around it. "What's going—?" Sherrie's sleepy voice began. Then the question was interrupted by a gasp of horror and indignation.

Sherrie stared another moment while Liza and Bill watched her in silent disbelief. Then she put a hand to her mouth, drew back into her room and slammed the door.

Liza let her head fall backward with the utter impossibility of trying to explain to her sister her compromising position in Bill's arms. She lay in his embrace like a corpse as he carried her into the room and dropped her unceremoniously onto the bed.

She sat up instantly. "Bill, you have to go explain it to her, right now."

He seemed to consider that course of action then dismiss it. "No. She won't believe me anyway, so let her stew over it."

"Bill!" Liza whispered, remembering the baby. "It'll be even harder to explain tomorrow!"

"Then we won't try," he returned quietly. He went to the crib, readjusted the baby's blankets, then went into the confined space behind the louvered doors.

"Don't do this," she pleaded, getting onto her knees so that she could turn and look at him through the open doors. "You know she loves you."

"Yes, I do," he said grimly. "But until she knows it, too, there's little hope for us."

"If you don't explain, there's *no* hope. And it ruins *my* relationship with her, too."

"Last night," he said wearily, pulling one of the doors closed, "you asked me to trust you. Tonight I'm asking you to trust me. That's fair, isn't it?"

She huffed a sigh and punched her pillow. "I'll kill you if you're wrong," she said.

He smiled grimly. "Good. 'Cause if I lose her, I'll want to die anyway. Good night." And he pulled the second door closed.

Chapter Six

Liza hurried down to the kitchen early, braced for combat. She'd done her bit for Bill by letting Sherrie stew overnight, but now she was determined to explain why she'd been in Bill's arms.

But Sherrie wasn't there. The bowl of flapjack batter stood on the counter along with a pound of bacon and a dozen eggs, and the griddle was on the stove, but there was no one in the room.

Liza peered out the window on the back door and saw the back of Sherrie's brown parka and cords in the middle of a world of white. She seemed to be staring at the leaden horizon.

Liza felt a terrible pain in the pit of her stomach at Sherrie's obvious distress. And at the knowledge that she'd caused it, however unwittingly.

She pulled on her boots and coat and went outside. The cold air slapped her in the face and took her breath away. She gave herself a moment to adjust, then trudged in Sherrie's direction.

A strong wind sent the snow flying off the trees in the yard, giving the morning a mystical atmosphere.

Liza had almost reached Sherrie when her sister spun around, one arm out in a halting gesture, stopping Liza in her tracks. "Don't even try," she said, her eyes and her voice as cold as the morning. "I won't listen."

Liza jammed her already frozen hands into her pockets, wishing she'd remembered gloves. "That's been your problem all your life, hasn't it? You don't listen. To anybody. You don't like your big dreams or your faulty conclusions muddled up with facts!"

"Don't you *dare* dissect my character," Sherrie ordered with a vicious jab of her index finger in Liza's direction, "when we're all in this hellish mess because of your big dreams and faulty little lies!"

"We're in this mess," Liza returned calmly, "so that Edie and I can keep our jobs, and so that you can buy the inn."

"Oh, fertilizer!" Sherrie shouted.

To anyone else, that insipid word for the real thing might have been amusing, considering Sherrie's passion at the moment. But Liza knew she used it to prevent the boys from picking up bad language, and had just fallen into the habit. Liza felt relatively sure a smile wouldn't be appreciated at the moment, anyway.

"We're in this mess," Sherrie shouted, "because you've enjoyed being the big Gouda, and you don't want to give it up. That's all."

"Sherrie," Liza said reasonably, "if I give it up, you give up a third of your income and your shot at the inn. Do you want to do that?"

"No!"

"Good. That's settled. Then do you want to hear about last night?"

"No, thank you." Sherrie pushed past her, headed back to the house. "I think the facts spoke for themselves on that issue."

Liza caught her arm and spun her around. "You misinterpreted what you saw!"

"*Tons* of fertilizer! I was willing to let the two of you sleep in the same room because your plan required it. You just didn't make it clear what lengths you'd go to to make it convincing!"

"Sherrie, Bill is sleeping in the closet!"

"Maybe, but apparently he carries you in there with him."

Sherrie tried to pull away from her, but Liza took hold of her with her other hand, too. "You nit! I got up with Betsy, then when she went back to sleep, I couldn't, so I went downstairs for a cup of tea, had a brief talk with Jeff, who was also up, and which totally tortured me because I know he's attracted to me but thinks I'm married and is too noble to do anything about it and neither can I or we all lose *everything*, but why should that bother you because you're in a jealous rage over a man you've claimed all along not to love!" Liza paused for a much-needed breath. Sherrie still glowered at her, but guiltily now. "Then we were both coming back upstairs when I tripped over Bill's robe—I forgot to bring mine, okay?—and Jeff caught me and carried me the rest of the way up the stairs. Bill apparently heard the commotion and came to investigate, at which point Jeff—thinking Bill is my husband—put me into his arms.''

Sherrie looked down at the snowy ground for a long time, then up into Liza's eyes. ''Really?'' she asked in a small voice.

Liza rolled her eyes. ''No. I made that all up on the spur of the moment.''

''I've heard you tell some very convincing lies since this all started.''

''Yeah,'' Liza admitted gravely, ''but never to you. Never in our lives to you.''

Sherrie looked at her a moment and her mouth began to quiver. ''All right. I'm sorry. I'm just...''

''Jealous.''

''Yeah. I guess.'' Sherrie sniffed back tears, then asked grumpily, ''Well, why didn't you come and explain this to me last night?''

''Would you have listened last night, or would I have just wasted my energy and awakened the whole household pounding on your door?''

Sherrie closed her eyes and sighed. ''I can't believe Bill didn't even try to explain.''

''You told him you don't want anything to do with him.''

''But we've meant a lot to each other.''

Liza tried to score one for his side. ''Well, you'll have to square that with him, but I think as the rules go, if you claim you don't care, then he's entitled to do what he wants to do without having to explain.''

''Fine. Then let him do that. I have flapjacks to

prepare." Sherrie stomped off toward the house, her boots biting into the snow.

Liza followed, thinking that not only did she have to somehow arbitrate this misunderstanding between Bill and her sister, she had to flip a flapjack while Mr. Whittier watched.

How could anyone, she wondered, have so much against them before seven in the morning?

BILL, JEFF, WHITTIER and the boys ate bowls of blueberries and bananas while Dora fed Betsy and Sherrie made flapjacks and placed them in the warming oven.

"Hurry up and use all the batter," Liza said to Sherrie under her breath as she placed a cup of coffee at her elbow. "We can claim you forgot to save one for me to flip."

"Sherrie!" Whittier called from the table. "Don't forget to save the last one so that Liza can demonstrate that skill she brags about in her column."

Liza groaned.

"You were saying?" Sherrie whispered with an amused glance.

"You could have spared me this," Liza accused dispiritedly, "if you'd worked a little faster."

Sherrie's smile was innocent. "The incentive just wasn't there." She removed a finished flapjack and put it in the oven. Then she sprayed the pan with oil, dropped in the last bit of batter and said softly, quickly, "I'll give it one turn, then you're on. The pan's well oiled, so it should go smoothly. Give it some Zen. Concentrate on where you want it to land.'' Sherrie turned the beautifully browned flap-jack, then called over her shoulder, ''Okay! Gather 'round. Liza's ready.''

Hoping that prayer and Zen were compatible, Liza employed both as she planted her feet squarely and held the handle of the pan in both hands.

The boys and Dora watched expectantly, Bill and Jeff stood with plates in hand, obviously watching simply to get seconds, but Whittier was in the spirit of the thing, clearly eager to see her pull off what she boasted about in his magazine.

Praying for and concentrating on a miracle, Liza flipped. She knew instantly she was off. The flapjack was high and outside. It turned beautifully in the air as though in slow motion.

She heard the collective gasp of her audience, Sherrie's whispered groan, and watched it begin to come down far beyond the reach of her pan.

Then Jeff reached up with his plate and caught it. It landed with a little slap and there was a moment's surprised silence.

''Right on target,'' Jeff said with a smile for Liza. ''Thank you. Are there a couple more to go with it?''

Whittier laughed, and everyone joined him. Bill and the boys asked for more, and the nerve-racking moment was over. No one seemed to have noticed that she hadn't accomplished what she'd claimed to do so expertly, only that Jeff had made a remarkable catch.

She sent him a grateful look, which he returned with a subtle nod.

Half an hour later Whittier looked almost comatose in his chair. Sherrie patted his shoulder as she topped up his coffee. "You don't look like you're going to be up to cutting holly and pine boughs this morning, Mr. Whittier."

Whittier leaned his head on his hand, the victim of too much breakfast. "It was the ninth flapjack that did it," he said. "Curse you women for being such brilliant cooks." He smiled weakly across the table at Jeff. "You and Bill and the boys will have to accompany Liza without me."

Bill shook his head. "Sorry. I have to run into the hospital for an hour or so."

"But you're on vacation!" Liza said. She voiced the complaint because she wasn't anxious to go off alone with Jeff now that she knew what it was like to be touched by him. Oh, the boys would be along, but they'd be running ahead, or lagging behind to explore, and she and Jeff would be *alone* and she'd want to stroke his cheek, touch his arm. And—even more dangerous—she'd be tempted to *explain.*

Fortunately, her complaint to Bill came off sounding like wifely concern rather than reluctance to go alone with Jeff.

"I know," he said with a husbandly pat on her shoulder, "and I won't be long, I promise. But the radiologist wants me to look at an ultrasound and I promised I'd come in. You can do this without me. Just let Jeff handle the clippers." He smiled at Jeff, clearly into his role this morning. "She ends up with a blood blister on the pad of her hand every time she uses them." He turned to the boys. "You be good for Mom. And no running off. You stay in sight."

"Sure, Pop," Travis said. "You know us."

"Yes. That's why I'm warning you. Davey?"

"Okay, Dad."

"Good." He ruffled the boys' hair and left the table. "Oh." He turned on his way out of the room, then came back, working a key off his key ring. "You'll need the truck." He handed her the key with a grin. "And be careful with it. It's dilapidated, but it's precious to me. And remember the rule. The boys will beg to ride in the bed, but they have to ride in the cab. Too many bumps."

Liza knew that was an issue every time Bill took Sherrie and the boys out in the truck.

"Of course," she said. "Don't worry. Be sure you're home for lunch. Sherrie's preparing my famous white chile."

He leaned down to kiss her cheek. "I wouldn't miss it. Have fun."

As he left the room, Liza reached for her mug to have another sip of coffee and discovered that Sherrie had taken it.

"I wasn't fin—" she began, but Sherrie either didn't hear her or chose to ignore her.

Whatever hope Liza might have had that Bill's warning to the boys guaranteed their good behavior was shot the moment she and Jeff went out to Bill's rusty old blue Chevy truck.

The boys were sitting in the bed.

"Come on," she said, walking around to the

driver's side. "You heard your father." She caught Travis's eye and winked. "Out of there and into the cab."

She opened the door and experienced a moment of panic when she spotted the gearshift. Oh, no. She couldn't drive a stick. Wouldn't Jeff find it strange that she couldn't drive her own truck?

"Do you mind if I drive?" Jeff asked, opening the passenger side door. He looked at her through the interior. "I haven't driven a vehicle since I was taken. I've traveled in planes, jeeps and limos, but I haven't gotten to drive."

"Oh, sure," she said, relief making her voice light. She tossed the key at him and grinned. "Just remember all Bill's cautions. I'd hate to have you survive kidnap and captivity only to die at the hands of an angry pediatrician."

He laughed, then reached up to lift Davey out of the back of the truck. "Out of there, you two. We're not going anywhere until you're in the cab."

Davey scrambled in next to the driver's seat as Jeff hauled Travis down.

When they were all in the cab, Liza pointed to the road beyond the stone wall that surrounded the yard. "Just follow that to the stream. It isn't far at all. We could walk it easily, but we'll need the truck to haul the greens back."

"Right."

Liza concluded that the boys were determined to make her look bad. Or their mother had instructed them to be as difficult as possible in revenge for the scene she'd misunderstood early that morning.

While she and Jeff walked among the cedars looking for healthy, low-hanging branches, the boys took the long clippers and a pruning hook and parried with them.

Liza took them away.

A little later she pointed out some likely branches to Jeff, then turned to find Davey chasing Travis with a broom Bill kept in the bed of the truck. Travis ran from him, carrying a hand saw.

"Travis! Davey!" she shouted. "Stop it!"

She chased them down and wrestled the tools from them. They were in a mood she'd seen only a few times before, too intent on their freedom to obey the rules. When Sherrie was in charge, the mood usually earned a well-placed swat and an evening without television, or an early bedtime.

She relieved each boy of his weapon and held the front of each jacket. "Don't you think for one minute," she warned firmly but quietly, "that I won't *act* like a mother and pound both of you if you don't settle down! I don't want you touching one of these tools unless you're asked, much less running with it. Now come back with me and do exactly what I tell you, or you will be grounded so long your grandchildren won't be able to go out! Do you understand me?"

"Jeez, Aunt Li—" Davey began.

Travis backhanded him in the stomach. "She's

Mom!" Then he frowned at Liza. "But you don't have to act like her. I like it better when you're nice."

"If *you* will be nice," she said, "I will be nice. Now, go to that tree where Jeff is and offer to help."

Jeff trimmed the bottom boughs off several of the shaggy white pines with their long, slender cones, and each bough was carefully carried back to the truck bed by Travis and Davey, who eventually fell into the routine.

"We could let them stack up," Jeff said, wielding the saw, "but this keeps them busy."

"Precisely." Liza took the branch he handed her and passed it on to Davey, who had run to her from the truck, eager for his next delivery. "The little savages."

"What are we going to use these for?"

"To decorate the table and to toss around the kitchen to make it look even more festive." She took a deep whiff of the air. "And it smells so wonderful. It's too bad we don't have smell-o-rama or something on television."

He laughed and sawed off another branch. "Your kitchen would draw every viewer—and nose—across the country. But I guess you manage to do that even without the aroma."

"Well. I was just lucky," she said modestly but honestly. "I had the right combination of things at the right time." Namely, her ability to write and her sister's expertise in the kitchen.

"Well, that's the American way. Find a need and fill it and become a happy capitalist."

Liza waved her cedar bough. "Power to the people." Travis appeared and relieved her of the bough, running to the truck with it.

"Tell me when we have enough." He moved on to the next tree. "I don't want to denude the woods."

"Oh, they're Bill's woods. Doctors get accustomed to nakedness." She dismissed that danger with a wave of her hand, then realized that his eyes were on her.

They went quickly back to his work, but not before she'd read the hot expression in them. He'd imagined her... denuded! She felt both excitement and alarm. His interest in her had taken a step forward. A giant step.

He'd shed his jacket, and she watched his shoulders move under the thick sweater he wore and saw an image behind her eyes of that back naked. She saw muscles stretch and ripple and imagined the narrowing line of his torso to his waist.

She closed her eyes to erase the image before it could go any further.

When she opened them again, Jeff was facing her, a pine bough held out. And she knew instantly that he knew why she'd closed her eyes.

Then something seemed to snap shut in him. She swore she almost heard the sound.

"Okay, guys," he said briskly as the boys returned. "Show me where the holly is."

Travis pointed back toward the house. "It's about halfway back."

They piled into the truck, and Jeff suggested Liza wait in it while he and the boys collected the holly.

"How much do you want?" The question was polite but completely without animation.

"Enough to fill two pots," she said, and showed him the width of the openings with her hands. "About this big."

"All right." He closed the door on her and headed off for the little cluster of glossy, red-berried holly trees.

The boys followed, talking nonstop while they worked.

Liza watched them, Jeff's concentration singular and suddenly brick jawed. He smiled at the boys and sent them back to the truck with small armloads of the prickly green, but didn't look once in Liza's direction.

She wasn't sure whether to be pleased or upset by his behavior. That little exchange about denuded trees had become something more without either of them intending it, and he seemed to be treating it like a danger signal.

She accepted that as a sign of an honorable man, and felt absolutely certain she was falling in love with Jeffrey James after less than twenty-four hours in his company. That seemed impossible, yet it was happening to her.

The question was, what could she do to cultivate that love in him when he had to continue to believe—at least for another day and a half—that she was a married woman?

Then it came to her. *Nothing.* She didn't have to do anything. He was forced to remain until the show was over. And the moment it was over, she could tell him the truth.

The problem would take care of itself.

She realized that might be a little optimistic, but it was Christmas. It was hard to be otherwise.

At least, it was until she and Jeff and the boys walked into the kitchen to find Sherrie screaming at Bill.

"That may be fine with you, but I didn't sign on to slave like a donkey while everyone else gets to have a high old time, morning, noon *and* night!" She slapped a tea towel on the counter with a vicious *whap*. "I'm just trying to make enough money to be independent of anyone else! All I ask is that my feelings be respected!"

Sure the entire scheme was seconds away from revelation, Liza cleared her throat.

Unfortunately Bill chose that moment to shout back. "You want your feelings respected while you stomp all over everyone else's?"

"And how did I do that?"

"Which time?" Bill demanded.

To Liza's horror, Whittier appeared in the doorway from the dining room.

"I have done nothing," Sherrie shrieked, "but cater to everyone's—"

Liza wasn't sure what did it, but something distracted Sherrie and she turned in the direction of the back door. At the sight of Liza, Jeff and her boys staring at her, she stiffened, her eyes widening with horror.

Liza watched Bill square his shoulders and step back into character—and take advantage of the moment. "Sherrie," he said with the calm authority one might use on an employee, "if Liza didn't value your skill so completely, and need your help so much right now, I'd tell you to find employment elsewhere. But you know we need you, so I suggest you store your grievances until after the show when we'll all have more time and patience to deal with them."

He nodded in the direction of their small audience. "Excuse me." He snatched a parka off the peg near the back door and went out into the snow.

The boys ran to Sherrie. "Mo—" Travis began, then stopped himself. "Aunt Sherrie," he said, putting his arms around her. "Are you okay?"

Sherrie took them into her arms and kissed each head. Tears had accompanied her outburst and she sniffed, tossing her hair back. "I'm fine. Did you and Jeff and your mom have fun collecting greens?"

"Yeah," Davey said. "But why was…why was Dad yelling at you?"

"Oh." She shrugged a shoulder. "Don't worry about it. Your dad and I fight all the time. We probably always will. Why don't you find something to do while I get lunch ready?"

"But…" Travis began to protest.

"Come on, guys." Jeff beckoned them toward him as he opened the back door again. "We'll get started on a snowman."

Davey ran off instantly, but Travis followed only after a concerned look back at his mother.

She shooed him away with a smile.

Whittier turned back in the direction of the living room, deciding, apparently, that Sherrie and Liza needed privacy.

The moment he was out of earshot, Sherrie went to the table and sat with her face in her hands. Liza sat beside her, rubbing gently across her shoulders.

"What happened?" Liza asked.

Sherrie dropped her hands to the table, her jaw set but her eyes miserable. "All I did was ask him about last night and he got all huffy."

"*How* did you ask?"

Sherrie obviously took offense to the question. "What do you mean, how? I said I thought he owed me an explanation."

"I had already explained to you."

"Yes, but he hadn't." Sherrie folded her arms stubbornly. "And even after he saw that I was upset, he didn't even bother to try. He just said that the two of you were playing the roles of a married couple, and he was finding it more appealing than he'd thought he would."

"Sherrie." Liza groaned impatiently. "Don't you see what he's doing? You're not giving him what he wants by admitting that you love him, so he won't give you what you want by admitting that nothing's going on behind that closed bedroom door."

"Well, he can just go to hell." Sherrie stomped off.

Liza watched her go, thinking that it was entirely possible hell was coming to them.

Chapter Seven

Jeff gave serious thought to leaving the house on the pretext of a late-afternoon walk, and not coming back. It wasn't that he didn't like the comfortable home and its volatile people—but that he did.

He'd never felt about a woman the way he felt about Liza De Lane. Even women he'd slept with. Even Sylvia.

Need for Liza was burning a hole in his gut. It was clouding his brain, clogging his thoughts, stealing his air, occupying every waking moment of his time—and many sleeping moments.

His only physical contact with her had been while she was wearing a heavy coat, and then last night when she'd worn flannel pajamas and a robe. Those could hardly be considered erotic moments. And other than that, all they'd done was talk, drive, walk, carry cedar boughs out of the truck to the back door.

Last night he'd blamed his reaction to her on several months of celibacy caused by his kidnap. Someone else might suggest that there was a certain appeal in her unavailability, but he refused to believe that.

Her married status didn't tantalize him, it tortured him.

Whatever the reason, he was going mad with wanting her. And he didn't just want her body, he wanted every sweet, hospitable, funny, kind, illogical inch of her.

But there was Bill.

He seemed like a loving husband and a devoted father, but something was going on between him and Sherrie that seemed too incendiary to be insignificant. Jeff felt reasonably sure that the argument they'd been having that morning had had less to do with employment than Bill had tried to make them believe.

Liza didn't seem to see that, however, or if she did, she didn't seem to care—and he found that difficult to believe.

No. There was some undefinable undercurrent moving in this idyllic home. And judging by the bubbling on the surface that morning, it was all about to explode. If it was going to mean Liza's freedom, he wanted to be there to catch her—and the boys.

The boys. He liked them. They were lively and bright and basically sweet hearted. That morning when they were giving Liza a hard time, they were just reacting to the rush of freedom such a pristine day encouraged. But they were the element that made an easy equation impossible.

If it was all going to fall apart between Bill and Liza, Jeff wanted to take Liza away. But the boys had a genuine and visible affection for their father, and

Bill's eyes betrayed love for them and Betsy. So how could he separate father and children?

The only alternative was separating mother and children, and he knew that couldn't happen. Liza wasn't much of a disciplinarian, but he could see how much she loved the boys and Betsy.

So a third alternative had been presenting itself, and he didn't like it. Bill and Liza had to figure out how they'd allowed Sherrie to get between them, and repair the situation.

But where did that leave Jeff?

Held hostage again, he realized. Only this time to his love for a remarkable woman.

So the invitation to a community dance being held that evening in a church hall was not particularly welcome news—to anyone.

The mayor of Rockbury, who also happened to be the pastor of the church hosting the dance, came in person to extend the invitation. He was a rotund little man in a gray overcoat with a sprig of mistletoe on his collar.

"Wonderful!" Whittier said with enthusiasm.

"And we'd be honored," the mayor said, after Bill had introduced him to Jeff and Whittier, "if you'd all come and join us. And you, Mr. James. You represent for us what the first Christmas was all about—lives rescued from bondage by the courage and generosity of one man."

Jeff put a hand to his heart. "Please, sir. Don't compare me to Jesus Christ."

The mayor smiled and clapped his shoulder.

"We're all called to be like Him, son," he said. "And we all know how hard it is, so when one of us does a remarkable job of it, it's time to celebrate. So, you'll all come?"

Bill turned to Liza. She looked pale. "You can all go ahead," she said. "I can't leave the children."

Dora stepped forward. "I'll look after them."

"But Betsy..."

"Is very happy when I put on that Baby Faces video and give her a handful of raisins. Please. Go."

Liza turned to the minister, obviously trying to create another excuse.

"Good," he said firmly. "Then we'll see you there. It's a potluck. Please bring whatever that is that makes the house smell so wonderful."

"I can't go," Sherrie said the moment the door closed behind the man. She strode purposefully toward the kitchen. "I have too much to prepare for tomorrow. And I still have to finish getting dinner...."

"You'll be fresher," Whittier cajoled, obviously anxious to take in the dance, "if you have a break. Besides, Liza's going to do all the work tomorrow, so you can finally relax a little, can't you? And the mayor said it's a potluck, so you won't have to worry about dinner tonight."

Sherrie swept a hand toward the boys. "The children still have to eat, Mr. Whittier."

"All *right!*" Travis said. "We can finally have those dinner-in-a-box things we bought that come with grape soda and chocolate chip pudding!"

Liza remembered that she and Sherrie had bought those to keep the boys happy during long days of food preparation. They had the fat content of a pound of butter, but Travis and Davey were thrilled with all the individual packets of bun, meat, cheese and dressing and the ability to put it all together themselves.

"Please! Please!" Davey joined his hands prayerfully and approached Sherrie. "Please go. If you do, Dora will let us stay up and watch whatever we want. Did you know she likes wrestling?"

Travis gave his brother a shove and a scolding look. "Some wheeler-dealer you are." Then he turned to Sherrie and said gravely, "If you go, we promise to watch only educational television, do some homework so we don't forget all about school over Christmas vacation and go to bed without complaint at nine-thirty."

Sherrie put a hand to her eyes. "I think that's a deal you should probably be making with your mother."

Travis was silent for an instant, then he cleared his throat. "Right," he said, and moved to face Liza. "What do you think, Mom? We'll watch the Discovery Channel."

She studied him with a grudging smile. "Really. And what's on the Discovery Channel tonight?"

He got the schedule from the coffee table and ran his finger down the grid until he located the channel.

"Um...sexual habits of the—"

"You know what?" Liza hugged the boys to her.

"You can watch wrestling. You're supposed to be on vacation from education, anyway."

"Cool, Mom."

"That's me."

SHERRIE WRAPPED UP the chicken pie—whose aroma the mayor had admired—and she and Jeff and Whittier piled into the back of Bill's Mercedes. Liza pulled down her sun visor and smiled at them through the makeup mirror.

"Everyone comfortable back there?"

Jeff forced himself to return her smile. He was sandwiched in between Whittier and Sherrie, who held the hot pie in its glass pan like a weapon to be used against anyone who got too close.

Whittier talked nonstop about doing the jitterbug as a young man when dancing involved body contact. "Those were the days," he said dreamily, "when you could hold a woman in your arms on the dance floor, and know by how she felt against you if this was something that could last a lifetime."

For Jeff, who'd spent most of the day suppressing a fiery longing and the memory of Liza in his arms, the man's reminiscences were like being worked over in a dungeon.

Liza looked over her shoulder to take exception to Whittier's statement, though she did it with a smile.

"That sounds pretty fifties, Mr. Whittier," she challenged. "You can't judge your compatibility with a woman for a lifetime by how she feels. You have to know what she thinks. What she believes."

"I didn't mean just the physical aspect of touching," Whittier amended. "I meant that a man can tell a lot by how a woman reacts to being touched. You know what I mean, Jeff?"

Of course he did—he just didn't want to go into it. But Liza and Whittier were watching him for an answer.

"I do," he said.

"Well, you explain it," Whittier said. "I have trouble with putting feelings into words. That's why I'm a publisher and not a writer."

"I'm an engineer," Jeff reminded him. "We measure things in fractions of fractions. Feelings defy that kind of close analysis."

"I disagree with that," Sherrie said.

Everyone looked in her direction, including Bill, who glanced at her in the rearview mirror. Then he turned off the quiet road onto a slightly busier thoroughfare. Welcome To Rockbury a sign said. Population 732.

"I think a woman measures a man's feelings for her every day," she said a little stiffly. "She even learns to gauge it against what kind of day he's had, how she feels, what's gone on in their lives to affect behavior." She sighed, the stiffening suddenly going out of her. She looked a little surprised and even embarrassed to find herself talking. "Anyway...we try to measure feelings all the time. I guess whether we do it correctly or not is another story." Then she turned to Jeff, her eyes quiet and just a little sad. "So I think an engineer can discuss feelings just like anyone else. What is it that a man can tell about a woman when he holds her in his arms?''

Since he wasn't going to get out of discussing it, Jeff tried to think it through. And the case in point—Liza in his arms—served as a clear example for him.

"Okay," he said, then caught Bill's eye in the mirror. "But feel free to jump in to help at any time."

"I'm staying out of this." Bill laughed. "You're the hero here."

"Go, Jeff," Whittier said, watching him as though he expected to learn something himself.

Liza waited, her profile turned toward Jeff. That was all the inspiration he needed.

"I think it happens in stages," he said. "There's a woman's initial reaction the moment you invite her into your arms. At that point, whatever her reaction, the situation remains liquid. She could be stiff or uncertain or receptive, but it could all change in a heartbeat."

Whittier raised an eyebrow. "Even if she's receptive?"

Jeff nodded. "One wrong move on your part and the second stage will end it all."

"The second stage?"

"Right. Her reaction to your reaction at having her in your arms." He waited a moment to make sure they were all with him. There was a collection of nods. "If she's an independent woman and you close your arms around her, she's on her way. If she's a woman who craves security and you choose to give her space and hold her too loosely, she's still on her way. Unless of course she finds something in you she relates to and she's willing to stay and see if you can still be what she needs. That takes you to the third stage.''

"You make it sound," Liza said, her eyes wide with fascination, "as though sexual interest *requires* an engineer."

"Well, obviously there's a difference between an engineer by profession," he said, "and an emotional engineer. Because you'll recall that my fiancée married someone else."

"Didn't she feel right in your arms?"

He thought back. Sylvia seemed to belong to another lifetime. "I seem to remember that I couldn't tell. She was restless and fidgety, so I left my arms open."

"Maybe she needed you to close your arms around her," Sherrie suggested softly.

"No," he replied. "I didn't want her to have to fight her way out."

Bill frowned at him in the mirror. "I want to hear about the third stage."

"That's the place Sylvia and I never got to. The place where you know it's right. When you can be sure she's happy there, that she wants to stay, and you can close your arms around her."

"If you never got there," Liza asked, her voice sounding breathless to his ear, "how do you know the third stage exists?"

"I guess I don't," he admitted.

"It exists," Bill said, turning the Mercedes into a very busy church parking lot. Out in the cold, crisp night people were talking and laughing and hurrying into the church, women holding their coats closed, men carrying covered dishes in boxes, bags and cleverly fashioned hand-sewn carriers. Bright lights and the sound of music came from the hall when someone opened the door.

But inside the Mercedes everyone was still strangely spellbound by their profound discussion. Bill turned off the motor, and the interior of the car was filled with silence.

"Of course," Whittier said, his voice quiet in respect for the moment, "you're a married man. You would know."

Jeff wasn't sure what told him, but he felt certain Bill's knowledge came not from his marriage but from something else. Or someone.

He didn't know whether that gave him hope or made him feel despair.

THE ROCKBURY Community Church's reception hall was festooned with garlands of greenery and twinkling lights. Couples in festive dress milled around in groups as women in aprons distributed the potluck offerings in order up and down the long tables—hors d'oeuvres and salads first, then entrées, followed by desserts.

There was a table with a punch bowl that gleamed under the lights, and another set up with coffee and tea, each manned by smiling ladies in aprons.

A band played romantic holiday music while everyone formed a line and made their way through the buffet line, then carried paper plates back to long tables covered with an unmatched collection of Christmas tablecloths.

Jeff felt the comfort and the old-fashioned warmth of his surroundings. A place like this, he thought, Sherrie and Liza in front of him in line, Bill and Whittier behind him, made him think that he might one day consider giving up the building of bridges and freeways for smaller engineering projects—like babies.

But the people who surrounded him with their love and generosity were the same people who were tearing him apart. Liza, whom he loved. And Bill, who also loved her, and whom Jeff liked and respected. And Sherrie, who was kind and helpful and who seemed to fit into their lives, but in no logical, workable way that he could see.

No. The best thing he could do for himself was to go back to Boston after the show and find a way to start over. Maybe he'd have to consider one of those deals Whittier was so sure would come his way. It would be bound to take him off in a new direction, and that was clearly what he needed.

Only... Christmas wasn't about doing for oneself. It was about seeing to what others needed, about giving love and sharing happiness. The trick was in trying to figure out how to do that when you had neither.

God. Being tied to a chair had been so much easier than this.

Jeff thought later that it might have all ended dif-
ferently if Bill hadn't asked Liza to dance, and if Liza
hadn't told him that her feet hurt. "Why don't you
ask Sherrie?" she said, apparently innocent of the romantic intrigue brewing around her. "She loves
'White Christmas.'"

Bill studied Liza a moment and Jeff couldn't help
but wonder if *he* wondered if she was on to him. But
no. The innocence seemed to be real. He'd have bet
she didn't have a clue.

Bill offered his hand to Sherrie, who sat on the
other side of Liza. "Sherrie? Would you like to
dance?"

She looked torn, as though she wanted to both accept and refuse.

"Go," Liza said to her under her breath, "so I can
have what's left of his chocolate cake."

Sherrie gave her that same suspicious look Bill had,
then accepted his hand and let him guide her onto the
dance floor.

Jeff looked away, unwilling to see Sherrie walk
into Bill's arms for fear of witnessing the third stage
of touch right there in front of Liza.

Whittier had left the table, and was dancing with
great style and enthusiasm with a long line of attractive older women.

"Your boss is having a good time," Jeff said, trying to distract Liza from her sister and her husband.

Liza swung her gaze to Whittier, dancing now with
a pretty, white-haired matron in a lacy red dress. "He
certainly seems to be. That's good. You said yourself

that Christmas should be about slowing people down, about reminding them of what's real in life. Have you noticed that he hasn't mentioned money, deals or audience share since we arrived?''

Jeff nodded, smiling at her ebullience. On the one hand, he wondered how a woman who seemed so bright and in touch with people and things could not even notice that her life might be falling apart. On the other hand, another side of him selfishly hoped it would, so that he could pick up the pieces.

''Are *you* having a good time?'' she asked him.

He had to lie. ''Of course I am. Why? Do I look unhappy?''

She studied him a moment, then replied with startling frankness, ''Yes, you do. And I should do something about that.''

He was almost afraid to ask. ''And what would that be?''

She stood and came around the table to catch his hand. ''I'm going to dance with you.''

Oh, no. ''But I thought you wanted Bill's chocolate cake?''

''I've changed my mind. I'm full.''

''Then…maybe we should sit this one out. What if you got leg cramps or…''

She gave him a smile with a frown in it. ''Jeff, that's for swimming.''

Well. He was floundering. ''But your…'' He'd started to protest that her husband might object, but Bill and Sherrie were looking into each other's eyes with an intensity Liza shouldn't see. ''Sure, why not?'' he said finally, letting her pull him toward the middle of the floor. "It's been a long time, though."

"It's like riding a bike."

"I had a skateboard."

She stopped in the swaying crowd of couples, her arms at her sides, her fingers still entangled with his, and gave him a devastating smile. "Must I remind you that it's considered polite to cater to the whims of your hostess?"

He thought it only fair to warn her. "Well, that's the trouble right there, Liza. I've never done well with whims. There aren't many capricious engineers. We're ruled by the laws of science and mathematics."

"But…an engineer's job," she said, "is to take the properties of matter and energy and make them useful, isn't it?"

"It is. But things only work within the rules that apply to matter and energy."

She smiled simply. "Jeff, this is only dancing."

He met her gaze and held it. "It isn't, Liza. And you know it isn't."

That was her chance to walk away, but she didn't take it, so he opened his arms.

She walked into them, and he knew before he even closed them around her that she wanted to be there, and that she wanted to stay. She leaned into him in a way that was entirely circumspect, yet disarmed him completely because her every move was unconscious and genuine.

She loved him; he was sure of it.

Reality crashed around him to the haunting melody

of "I'll Be Home for Christmas." Not only did she
love him, but she wanted him to know it.

She, Liza De Lane, who was married to Bill
McBride and had three children. And on December
23, the day before Christmas Eve, she was practically
saying the words.

All right, he decided. They were going to settle
this.

Liza knew her behavior was reckless, but Whittier
was so busy being the gallant with the older population of Rockbury's ladies, and Bill and Sherrie desperately needed private time together, and she
couldn't have waited another minute to be in Jeff's
arms.

And it was everything she remembered. Everything
she'd dreamed. When his arms closed around her, life
suddenly made sense. There *had* been a purpose to
all the wild and challenging machinations of this
Christmas in Connecticut. The man who'd used an
image of her to get himself home now made a home
for her in his embrace.

She looked into his eyes and saw love there. Joyful
and completely distracted, she let her role of wife and
mother slip and let him see what lay under the
guise—the Liza De Lane who was very much in love
with him.

Without warning, he dropped his arms from around
her, caught her hand and led her off the dance floor
and toward the front door. He stopped at the long rack
crammed with coats and scarves in the vestibule of

the hall, obviously trying to spot his parka and her red coat.

He walked around the rack to the second rod, still searching. Liza heard a startled exclamation and a little scream of surprise. She started around the rack of coats and collided with a grim-faced Jeff.

He turned her physically around and pushed her before him back around the rack and toward the door. He stopped her to help her on with her coat.

"Jeff, what's the matter?" she asked. But he shrugged silently into his own coat, then opened the door.

They were hit by a blast of cold air and swirling snow.

"Sleigh rides, ten dollars," a man dressed as an elf shouted from the front of the parking lot. "Let Santa drive you through the woods. Only ten dollars!"

"Come on." Jeff caught her arm and pulled her with him toward the sleigh. A very rotund figure garbed in red wool and white fur and wearing the classic Santa hat sat in the front, hands on the reins of a horse-drawn sleigh. "How long's the trip?" Jeff asked.

"Half an hour," the elf replied.

Jeff pulled a wallet out of his inside coat pocket and handed the elf a twenty-dollar bill.

"We want it to take an hour."

The elf pocketed the bill. "You got it. Gentleman wants an hour trip, Santa Stan."

"Ho, ho," Santa Stan replied with a distinct lack of enthusiasm.

Jeff helped Liza into the sleigh then climbed in beside her. He pulled a red-and-green-plaid woolen blanket up over her, then, noticing that her head was bare, drew the hood of her coat up to cover her.

"Go, Santa," he called. He put an arm around Liza, tucking the blanket around her shoulders, and the sleigh started off into the lightly falling snow.

Jeff's arm around her was the first real clue Liza had that something had gone very wrong with the snug scenario she'd created.

"Do you want to tell me what happened?" she asked a little nervously.

"Not yet," he said, glancing over his shoulder.

Liza looked, too, and saw nothing.

"I'll tell you when we're out of town," he said. He watched her tuck her hair into the side of her hood and caught her bare hand in one of his. "Don't you ever carry gloves?" he asked.

Without waiting for an answer, he delved into his coat pocket and drew out the brown lined leather gloves Bill had lent him and helped her put them on.

She wanted to insist that he tell her what had troubled him, but his sudden change of mood from the courteous, respectful guest to authoritative man-in-charge was exciting and she hated to do anything that would change things back.

She sat beside him, enjoying his arm around her, as the sleigh cut its smooth way through the snow down Rockbury's main street, then made a turn that led them down a quiet little lane flanked by woods on both sides.

Every branch was topped with snow, and more drifted down with quiet beauty onto the trees, the road, the horse and Santa Stan.

Widely spaced streetlights illuminated the straight ribbon of lane ahead and Liza waited patiently for Jeff to explain himself, thinking that she wouldn't mind if this ride went on forever. Except that something must have happened to make him so suddenly and physically protective.

The horse clopped along, his hooves the only sound on the quiet lane. Santa Stan guided him with very little movement, making no effort to communicate with Jeff and Liza, seemingly lost in his own world.

"Do you love Bill?" Jeff asked without preamble.

Liza's brain worked furiously. She'd thrown caution to the wind tonight, but how far was she willing to go with this? She wanted him to know the truth, but not quite yet. And tonight—the night before the show—was probably not the best time for revelation.

"Well…yes," she said finally, not at all surprised by his dark frown.

He shook his head. "If you were married to me I'd sure as hell want more enthusiasm than that from you."

She indulged herself by concentrating on that possibility briefly. Then she turned her attention back to the moment. "Why do you ask?"

He looked at her closely, as though judging her ability to withstand what he was about to say. What on earth had happened?

"Because…" He tried to go on, then faced forward

again, obviously deciding to change his approach. "I keep telling myself this is none of my business," he said, his jaw set, his brow furrowed. "But you mean a lot to me, and you don't seem to have a clue about what's going on. And the only way I can save you from being kicked is to say it clearly."

"So far," she said with a teasing smile, "you're not doing a very good job of that."

He turned to her, his eyes dark and apologetic. "Your husband and your sister are fooling around on you."

She gasped in shock, not for the reason he thought, but because they'd all been so careful about their little charade.

"I'm sorry." He rubbed the shoulder of her red wool coat. "I've been noticing their smoldering looks at each other since I arrived, but when I got our coats...I found them kissing behind the rack."

Liza remembered the surprised exclamation she'd heard, the little scream of alarm. So that was what had changed Jeff into her champion.

Her brain revved to warp speed, weighing her options. But considering it didn't even always work well at ordinary speed, she wasn't surprised when she had difficulty deciding what to do.

Should she let him believe her "husband" and her sister were having an affair? Believing that had brought about the most wonderful change in him. And she had to think it was because he wanted to be the one to replace Bill in her affections.

He took her unfocused stare for shock and tucked

the blanket more tightly around her, holding her firmly in his arm.

"I'm sorry," he said again as the sleigh moved on up the snowy road. The lights were only occasional now, and she thought distractedly that the darkness seemed less friendly than it had when they'd set out. "I can only imagine how much it hurts, but you're going to have to deal with it before the boys notice. The way Bill and Sherrie were acting tonight, it's just a matter of time before all of Connecticut knows."

Liza closed her eyes against the guilt creeping over her. He was thinking about Travis and Davey, not himself.

"Fortunately, I think Whittier's been too excited over the prospect of the show to see anything. And tonight the lovely Rockbury matrons have kept him preoccupied." He squeezed her to him. "I know the night before the show's a rotten time to tell you, but Bill and Sherrie seem to be losing their sense of discretion. I was afraid you'd find them in some clinch in a corner tomorrow and be too upset to go on." He leaned his head against hers for a moment. "This way at least you'll have a little time to deal with it and prepare yourself."

Liza still couldn't speak.

"Are you all right?" he asked when all she could do was stare at him. Somehow, at the conception of her plan, she hadn't foreseen this eventuality—the man she'd come to love being all kindness and understanding because he thought her "marriage" had fallen apart. "Liza, please say something."

She said in complete honesty, "I...I don't know what to...do."

"Of course you don't," he sympathized. "I guess your first consideration should be..." He hesitated, as though saying the words was difficult for him. "Whether you love him enough to try to save the marriage. If all the two of you have invested means more to him than Sherrie does, and if it means enough that you'd be able to forgive him—and her—and go on."

Liza looked into his eyes, wondering if she'd completely misunderstood his reaction to the situation. He hadn't once mentioned his place in it.

"Does the outcome matter to *you?*" she whispered.

His blue eyes looked into hers, clearly in pain. "Of course it does. I want you to be happy, whatever that takes."

"With him," she asked, her voice barely there, "or with you?"

His eyes registered the added pain of her question. "If it was just you and me involved, I'd say leave the bum tonight." His expression hardened as he accepted the facts. "But you have three children who love Bill to think about. And...if I was to think about it without considering my interests here, I'd say..." He groaned, and went on grudgingly, "I'd say, Sherrie aside, Bill does seem to adore all of you. Maybe it was just a one-time thing. Maybe he had some problem he couldn't bring to you with the show coming up and he...sort of...lost it. Maybe a good no-holds-barred talk between the two of you could straighten everything out."

Then because the past few days had been terribly stressful on many levels, and because he displayed more moral fortitude than Liza could ever hope to have—thus making it clear to her that she didn't deserve him anyway—she burst into tears.

Unable to draw breath and explain, Liza buried her face in Jeff's shoulder. He wrapped both arms around her and let her cry, thinking, she was sure, that her outburst was in reaction to the news that he'd caught Bill kissing Sherrie.

She had to straighten that all out, of course. And she had to do it tonight. She couldn't let him believe Bill was the kind of man who'd cheat on a woman, or that Sherrie was the kind of sister who would betray her.

But right now she didn't know how to put all that into words, so she didn't even try. She just wept at all she was probably going to lose when she finally did.

It was some time later when she noticed that the lane had grown considerably rougher.

"Hey!" Jeff shouted. "Stan! We're off the road! Stan?"

Liza looked up to see that they'd turned onto an unpaved road in the woods. The horse, apparently spooked by the eerie sound of the wind in the trees and the snow blowing across their path, had picked up speed.

The confined space prevented him from a serious

gallop, but he was moving fast enough to cause concern for the sleigh's runners in the tightly grouped trees.

Santa Stan didn't respond to Jeff's shouts.

Jeff threw himself forward over the front of the sleigh, reaching for the reins. He swore, and Liza took that to mean that Stan no longer held the reins and that they'd fallen out of reach.

But that problem was solved for them a moment later when the left runner hit a tree, yanking the horse off his feet and flinging the sleigh sideways so that the back of it hit another tree.

As Liza held on for dear life, Jeff flew out into the snow, landing with a thud that was very loud in the sudden stillness.

Liza threw the blanket off and stood, staring in horror at the picture highlighted even in the darkness by the white snow that overlaid everything. There was the horse on its side, struggling to rise, and Santa Stan, lying in a heap in the bottom of the sleigh. She looked at the crumpled runner half torn away from the vehicle—and at Jeff, lying inert against a tree as snow began to fall in earnest.

Chapter Eight

"Jeff! Jeff! Oh, darling, *please* be alive." Liza whipped off an oversize glove and patted snow onto Jeff's brow and cheeks. "Jeff? Jeff! Oh, God!"

It was all her fault. Liza leaned over him and put her hand to his mouth. She almost wept with relief when she felt his breath against it. She ran her hands over his body, looking for broken bones. Wouldn't it be in keeping with the way everything had been going for him to have escaped terrorists by the skin of his teeth only to end up dead of a head injury thanks to her and a sleigh and a Santa named Stan?

Stan. Liza looked back at the sleigh where Stan's arm hung over the front. Had he had a heart attack? she wondered, her panic increasing. God! How was she going to explain a sleigh ride in the woods that had resulted in two lifeless bodies!

She tore her coat off and placed it over Jeff, then went to the sleigh to try to assess Stan's condition. She didn't need daylight to reach a diagnosis.

It became obvious immediately thanks to the loud

snores and the odor of cheap alcohol issuing from his slack mouth. Santa Stan was in a drunken sleep!

With a cry of anger Liza punched his shoulder and ran back to Jeff.

"Jeff!" She dabbed more snow on his face. "Jeff, honey, please! I love you so much!"

She saw a wince on his face, heard a groan come from deep in his throat, then watched his hand come up to rub the back of his head.

Liza had never seen or heard anything so beautiful in her life.

"Jeff!" she said again, putting an arm around him to help him sit up. "Jeff, are you okay? Say something! Are you all right?"

"What...happened?" he asked, brushing snow off his face. "Where are...?" He stopped as his eyes tried to focus in the darkness. "God. It feels like Beirut again."

"No," she assured him quickly, rubbing at the back of his head. "We were taking a sleigh ride...."

"Oh, yeah." He groaned again and tried to get to his feet.

Liza pushed him back again. "Just sit for a minute," she ordered, casting a disparaging glance back at Santa Stan. "Santa's all right. He's drunk!"

Jeff turned his head gingerly from side to side. "Yeah. I smelled it on him when I reached over him to get the reins. Is ...the horse all right? Why's he neighing?"

Liza realized for the first time that the horse was making a considerable amount of noise.

"He fell on his side when we crashed," she said, holding Jeff's arm and putting a supporting hand to his back as he got carefully to his feet.

Her coat slipped off him and he grabbed it up and handed it back to her. "Put it on."

He leaned on her for support and dug in to his pants pocket. He produced keys and a little puddle of light from a flashlight on the ring.

He went to the horse and flashed the light over the harness, then had Liza hold it while he unfastened him from the sleigh. Once free, the horse drew his legs under him and pushed to his feet, mercifully uninjured.

Jeff looped a couple of fingers into the bridle. "Whoa, Rudolph," he said quietly, patting his neck to calm him. "Everything's okay. Whoa."

He drew a breath as though to try to clear his head and looked around at the weirdly light late-night landscape.

"Okay," he said. "What have we got? Cell phone?"

"In my purse at the dance," Liza replied.

"All right. So nobody's coming to us. We have to get back to them." He patted the horse. "Don't go anywhere, Rudolph. We're going to need you."

"Rudolph?"

"He was pulling a sleigh, wasn't he?"

"Cute. But what are we going to need him *for?* The sleigh's creamed. It's not going anywhere."

"Yeah, well, this is starting to look like a blizzard. Here. Hold him." He wound her fingers in the bridle as he'd done, and noted her bare hand again. "Where's the glove?" he asked crossly.

She pointed to where he'd fallen. "I wanted to feel if you were breathing."

He snatched up the glove, hesitated a moment to put a hand to his head as he straightened, then handed it to her.

"Dizzy?" she asked worriedly. "Maybe you have a concussion. Maybe we should just sit—"

"No time to sit. We have to get Santa under cover and get moving."

The horse reared his head and almost lifted her off the ground.

"Hold him firmly!" Jeff snapped at her.

"All right!" she returned in the same tone. "Jeez. Are you always this crabby when you regain consciousness?"

"On my own," he replied, "I seldom find myself rendered unconscious."

"You'll recall that this sleigh ride was your idea," she said testily, surprised by his mood and a little frightened by their circumstances.

He gave her a look she couldn't interpret, except to know that it wasn't friendly, and went to the sleigh. She watched as he pushed it with great effort farther into the trees where the branches were so thick and closely entwined that the snow fell thinly.

He patted Santa down and found a pocketknife. He covered him with the blanket they'd used in the back of the sleigh, then laboriously cut off several broad branches of pine and laid them atop the blanket.

"To hide him?" Liza asked.

He frowned at her. "To keep him warm until we can get to town and send someone back for him. I thought you were a country woman."

Annoyed with herself because she should have known that, she ignored him and stroked the horse's nose.

With Santa Stan snoring loudly through his cocoon of pine boughs, Jeff went back to Liza and the horse.

"Do you ride?" he asked.

Knowing she was about to defeat herself again, Liza expelled a breath. "In a car, yes. On a horse, no. If that's what you're getting at. Besides, he doesn't have a saddle."

With a grumbled oath, Jeff took a fistful of mane, leapt and landed astride Rudolph.

Liza stared at him openmouthed, hoping he wasn't expecting her to do that.

He leaned sideways off the horse and caught her around the waist. "Hold on," he said. "It's been a while since I stole a woman this way."

She felt his fingers bite into her waist even through the bulky coat, then she was lifted off the ground and onto the horse. As he positioned her in front of him, she thanked the fates that had led her to choose the green pants outfit over the slim-skirted red dress when she got ready tonight.

"Which way do we go?" Liza asked, confused by the sameness of trees in every direction.

He pointed to the shallow ruts the runners had

made in the snow. "Those'll work for us, at least until we reach the road."

"Why not after we reach the road?"

"The snow's falling pretty heavily. They'll be obliterated. You *sure* you grew up in the country?" He tightened his knees and the horse went forward at an easy walk. The same gesture also tightened on her thighs, tucked above his, and she remembered with sudden, alarming clarity that just before the crash he'd been trying to help her save her marriage. The one that didn't exist yet somehow stood between her and him as stoutly as a ten-foot wall.

"I spent most of my time in the kitchen," she said weakly. "Remember that it was my apricot-glazed ham that led you home, not my ability to track small game."

"And the way you looked in the gingham apron."

"That's sexist."

"I admitted that it was."

"But you don't feel you have to apologize for it?"

She heard his light laugh against the side of her hood. "No. I realize it's no longer a popular concept, but I can't help it. I spend a lot of time in wild, uncomfortable country, and when I fantasize about a woman, I see her as warm and plump and welcoming."

"But the way you described Sylvia..."

"Sylvia's kind of a law unto herself," he said. "A curious mixture of old-fashioned and contemporary. She's a great cook and always studying and testing to learn something new. But she has to have things her way or not at all.''

They'd reached the road, and out from under the shelter of the trees, Liza could see that it was near-blizzard conditions. There was no evidence of the trail the runners had left.

She pointed to the left. ''That way. We turned right into the woods.''

Jeff pointed in the other direction. ''We turned left. Besides, you were crying and not looking.''

''But I *felt* the turn.''

He made a disbelieving sound. ''Yeah, right. You don't know which direction is which when you can *see* it.''

She turned to look at him over her shoulder, having to move her hood aside to frown at him. ''There's no call to be mean.''

''I'm not being mean. But if we follow your sense of direction, we'd better know how far away the next town is.''

''It's twenty-one miles. And if we turn left we'll get to Rockbury, not to Oak Meadows.''

''We could get pretty hypothermic in twenty-one miles,'' he said.

''But we won't,'' she insisted, ''because it's only about three miles to Rockbury, and it's that way.'' She pointed firmly left.

''All right.'' Jeff urged Rudolph to turn left onto the road and huddled into his coat collar as they headed for Rockbury.

Only, Rockbury was in the other direction. That

became clear after more than half an hour when they passed a ramshackle cabin and barn in a clearing off the road.

Jeff pulled the horse to a stop. "I don't remember that from the sleigh ride," he said.

The air was absolutely frigid, the snow was blowing into her hood, her collar and up her coat, and making visibility difficult. "I don't, either," she admitted reluctantly. "I guess I was...mistaken."

"You mean wrong?" he asked, urging the horse toward the buildings.

"Mistaken. Wrong. What's the difference?" she asked testily. "*You* listened to me."

"I did," he said. "Because you've lived here for seven years and I've never been to Connecticut in my life. What was I thinking?"

Liza was beginning to wonder if he was schizophrenic. For two days she'd seen the charming, sensitive side of him and now suddenly he was impatient and sarcastic. A corner of her mind not numbed with the cold realized that wasn't an entirely fair assessment, considering she'd just guided him in the wrong direction in abominable conditions in a potentially dangerous situation, but she was tense and frightened and not anxious to own up to the fact that it was all her fault.

He guided Rudolph into a barnlike structure that was ancient but appeared to be sound. Jeff flashed the small light around, revealing several stalls. The horse went into one as though surprised and delighted to find comfortable accommodations.

Jeff lowered Liza to within a few inches of the ground, then let her go. She landed lightly but didn't budge, unable to see a thing.

Jeff swung his leg over Rudolph's head and leapt down beside Liza, shining the puny light into the corners of the stall. She heard scurrying sounds and saw curious movements of the straw on the barn floor.

"Stay right here," Jeff said. "I'm going to look around and see if I can find something for Rudolph to eat."

"But...there's things moving around..." she protested, sidling closer to the horse.

Jeff had started across the barn, but his voice came dryly out of the darkness. "They won't hurt you. I'm sure they have you pegged as a country girl."

"I'm getting tired of your sarcasm!" she shouted, mostly to hear the sound of her own voice as his footsteps retreated into blackness.

There were a few long moments of silence, except for subtle rustling noises across the barn. Then Jeff's light reappeared, followed by his tall form in the out-of-place overcoat.

"Found some hay," he reported, placing a bale of it at the horse's feet. "This place is in use by somebody. The hay is fresh. Someone must have used this building in the fall." He took a clump of straw from the floor and used it to rub down Rudolph. "There you go," he said, patting the horse's flank. "Not exactly blue-grass quality, but it'll tide you over until morning."

He caught Liza's arm and pulled her out of the stall. "Here. Hold your arms out."

"Why?" she asked.

He placed a length of wood in her outstretched arms. "Firewood." He followed that chunk of wood with several more, caught a few in his arms, then led the way out of the barn and turned toward the cabin, with the small swath of his penlight leading the way.

It was just enough to pick out several steps, a bench that had fallen over, and a door hanging lopsidedly on its rickety hinges.

"I wonder how old this is?" Liza thought aloud as Jeff's light illuminated a small, rough stone fireplace inside. The single room had shelves in one corner that might have served as a kitchen, and pegs along the other side where a bed might have stood.

"Very old would be my guess," Jeff replied, going toward the fireplace. He dropped the wood on the floor beside it and instructed her to do the same. "Middle of the last century, maybe. I can't believe your historical society hasn't restored it, or that some beautification organization hasn't torn it down."

"Maybe it still belongs to someone." Liza watched him run the light atop a rough, dusty mantel. "What are you looking for?"

"Matches," he replied.

"Are old matches still going to work?"

"Someone obviously uses the barn. I thought they might come into the old cabin to…" His hand slapped down on something and he said triumphantly, "You're good, James. You're really good." He held the light to several books of matches. "Rockbury To-bacconist," he read from one of them. "Oak Meadows Bar and Grill and The Fox Club in New York. Hmm. A traveler."

He struck one of the matches against the strip on the back of a book. There was a sizzling sound, then the bright light of a flame.

He held it up and ran it over a rough wooden box on the floor. He kicked it open with his foot, then grinned.

"The fates are with us, Liza. Kindling and newspaper."

"All *right!*" she said. "Warmth!"

In a few moments a smoky fire was burning in the fireplace and Jeff used one of the logs they'd brought in to nail the hinge back in place so that the door would close. There was still a drafty gap on the bottom, but he stuffed it with crumpled newspaper. He'd carried in the bench from the front porch.

He looked around at the reasonably snug cabin and nodded. "Now, if the elf went looking for Santa when he didn't return, we'll all make it through the night."

Liza put a hand to her mouth in sudden horror. She'd been so involved in their efforts to get back to Rockbury that she'd forgotten what her faulty directions meant to Santa Stan.

"Oh, my God!" she said. "What if they don't find him?"

"They will. And he was pretty well bundled up." He pointed her to the fire. "Sit down and try to get warm. As soon as it's daylight, we'll head off in the other direction. We should make Rockbury in no time.''

Her concerns for the alcoholic Santa were suddenly crowded out by how Sherrie and Bill and the boys would worry when she and Jeff didn't return tonight. And Whittier would be on the verge of apoplexy at the thought that his Christmas special wouldn't be made after all.

"Liza, I know what you're afraid of." Jeff pushed her onto the bench he'd placed before the fire, then got down on one knee on the floor and held his bare hands out to the flames.

Liza's battered instincts told her that a new hook was about to form in her already barbed ball of lies. "What?" she asked.

"You're afraid that when we don't come home tonight, Bill will think you stayed with me to get back at him for what I saw, and that it'll destroy whatever chance you might have had to pull your marriage back together."

She shook her head, parting her lips to protest that that wasn't at all what worried her, but he pushed himself to his feet and sat beside her. The intensity of his expression robbed her of speech.

"Don't worry. The damaged runner on the sleigh and the condition of Santa Stan will prove that it was an accident." He smiled thinly, grimly. "And if Bill's been married to you for twelve years, he has to know what a poor sense of direction you have. Convincing him that you got us lost should be a cinch."

She was desperate with the need to tell him the

truth, but the words were lodged in her throat and refused to be spoken.

He wrapped his arms around her and held her close. "I know," he said gently, his lips at her ear. "If he loves you, he'll listen."

Her high, shrill scream surprised her as much as it surprised him. She pushed her way out of his arms and got to her feet.

"Liza," he said calmly, standing with her. "Take it easy. It's going to be..."

She spun around to face him, yanking her hand out of his grasp, and found herself half-blinded by the side of her hood. She swiped it off her head with an angry gesture.

Then, remembering a little belatedly that this was all her fault and not his, she forced herself to take a breath. But it didn't seem to calm her. Nothing, she thought fatally, could calm her now.

"Jeff, I have to tell you something," she blurted out, pointing him back to the bench. "Sit down."

"Liza..." he began.

"Jeff, please!" she said too loudly.

He frowned at her worriedly, but he sat.

"I..."

He waited, the picture of tolerance in the shadowy room. That seemed to further entangle the words she struggled so hard to say.

"I'm not..." A sob rose in her throat, but she swallowed it and made herself speak the truth. "I'm not married to Bill McBride. I never have been."

For a moment he did not react. Then he shifted on

the bench as he seemed to try to make sense of her statement.

"You're not married to Bill," he repeated, as though he had to hear it a second time.

"That's right," she confirmed.

"The children..." he began, still seeming more confused than angry.

"Are Sherrie's."

"Sherrie's."

She couldn't blame him for needing to hear everything twice. "Yes. She's divorced from their father. She...she's the one who loves Bill and should be married to him."

Jeff held her gaze, confusion now beginning to lose ground to anger, though his voice remained quiet. "Then why the charade?"

She pulled her coat tightly around her and held it there by folding her arms over it. She *was* cold, but the feeling was coming from inside her, not from the drafty cabin.

"It's very complicated," she said.

"I'm reasonably intelligent," he countered stiffly.

She put a hand to her eyes as she thought back over how it had all begun and realized how completely ridiculous it would sound to someone else, particularly someone who'd been unfairly used by her ploy.

She told him how she'd gotten the job with *Wonder Woman Magazine* in the first place.

"I couldn't find a straight reporting position anywhere," she explained, trying to make her desperation at that time clear without sounding self-pitying. "I'd been out of work for four months and my savings were gone. So I heard the magazine was looking for a country columnist, and I applied. The managing editor was a friend of mine from my weekly newspaper days right out of college, and she *knew* I had no cooking or homemaking skills and that faking it would be harder than I thought. But she respected me as a writer, and when I got the idea that Sherrie could collaborate with me from Connecticut, she went for it. Whittier had been on her for weeks to hire someone."

Jeff stared at her, then stood and took several steps away from her, stopping at the edge of the shadows to look back at her in obvious puzzlement. "Okay, maybe I'm not as intelligent as I thought. How did that result in a phony husband and children?"

Liza spread her arms helplessly. "I don't know, I guess I just...really got into it. Bill's been the kids' pediatrician for years, and I think he's secretly loved Sherrie all that time. When Tom left her for a woman he worked with, Bill saw his chance and took it. He found every pretext in the world to get Sherrie to come to his home, including hosting the boys' birthday parties for her because she didn't have the room in her duplex. I came to one of them and fell in love with the house." She waved a hand in the general direction of Rockbury. "The house where you're staying *is* Bill's house."

Jeff pointed in the opposite direction. "It's that way."

"Does it matter?" she demanded impatiently. "I'm trying to tell a story here."

"It seems to matter," he replied quietly. "You seem to do the same with right and wrong as you do with east and west. You get them confused."

"It wasn't deliberate," she said in self-defense. "It just sort of happened. I created a country persona for myself using Bill's house as my...base camp. I imagined all I'd do if I lived there, and fortunately Sherrie, who's always been a Suzy Homemaker type, was able to make me sound credible. Tom had just left her and cleaned out their savings, and I shared with her, so it worked out for both of us."

"That still doesn't explain Bill and the kids."

She smiled grimly. "Sherrie and I have always been a good team. And we wrote the hell out of that column. Readers wrote me wanting to know more, hungry for the details of my life because they related to the warm and cozy world I'd created in the Connecticut countryside. Obviously I couldn't tell them I was writing it from my high-rise in Manhattan, so I assumed Sherrie's life—only a more perfect version of it. What it would be like if she was married to Bill."

He walked the perimeter of the cabin, cloaked by the shadows. She turned toward him, following his movements with her eyes. "It worked beautifully. We were asked to do a local cable show last Christmas and filmed it in a studio I had a friend set up for me. Whittier was in Europe at the time, and only Edie and the crew she hired knew that it wasn't really my home. I brought Sherrie in as my assistant, she got everything ready beforehand, and we pulled it off. That was the show you saw.''

He paced across the back of the cabin. She followed the sound of his footsteps. "That show did so well that when Whittier was approached with using me for a national network show that would be shot at my home and include my husband and my children, he took the deal without bothering to ask me, certain I'd be thrilled at the prospect of national exposure.''

"And you were," he guessed, "so you pulled together a cast of characters to deceive your viewing public?"

She swallowed hurt feelings, certain he had every cause to presume that was true. "No. But the deal was done, and telling the truth would have meant Edie's job and Sherrie's share of my job. Also, Sherrie's half of the money offered me for the show would enable her to buy the inn where she works as chef. She would love that independence. Tom's long gone and hasn't sent her a dime.''

He came to the edge of the shadows, his dark overcoat blending into the darkness, only his face set in angry lines emerging like some moral judge.

"So your motives were noble," he said. "Is that what you're telling me?"

"Not entirely," she admitted. "I did it also because I saw the interview with you on television, and...when you said that my face had brought you home..." She had to swallow before she added, "I fell in love with you.''

Chapter Nine

Jeff stepped fully out of the shadows, his expression openly skeptical. "And to show your love you invited me to your home and proceeded to lie to me on every possible level? I don't think so."

Liza sank wearily onto the floor in front of the fire, pulling off her shoes and holding her stockinged feet toward the flames. "Well," she said, feeling everything she'd hoped for for herself and Sherrie dissolve into nothingness, "I can't control what you think. You have to believe what you want to believe."

She heard him walk up behind her, but she didn't turn or look up.

"You expect me to believe," he asked, "that you felt something for a face you saw for sixty seconds on television?"

She stared into the flames. "Isn't that what you did? But with you, my face only made you risk your life. In my case, I risked my feelings, my heart."

He was silent for a moment, then she heard him sit on the bench. "Very poetic, but I don't buy it. I think you invited me onto your show because it would mean more viewers and ultimately more money.''

"Whittier invited you onto the show before he even told me," she corrected flatly. "All I was offered was a flat sum that would have been the same whether or not you appeared."

"Well, I'm sure your agent has you well protected."

"I don't have an agent," she denied with a sigh. "I'm just a columnist. Though probably not for much longer. I imagine you'll be leaving before the show?"

Escape had been Jeff's first instinct. And why not, he asked himself. He was good at it.

But he was getting tired of running away from people who held him hostage for their own purposes. With the Fatwa Jihad, he and Father Chabot had been political pawns in a mad and hopeless game. He'd had no choice but to run.

But he'd be damned if he was going to be chased away this time by a woman in a gingham apron—one who'd tortured him with her warmth and kindness and let him believe she belonged to another man.

He would make her pay for turning the Christmas he'd fought his way home to into some surreal Halloween.

He considered his options.

When he didn't answer, she turned that sweet face up to him, her eyes sad and weary, her hair tumbled.

He leaned forward, resting his forearms on his knees. That brought them face-to-face.

"Maybe we can cut our own deal over this," he

suggested, ignoring the conscience that tried to interfere with his revenge.

She looked into his eyes, suspicious of his intentions. "What are the terms?"

"I'll stay and do the show," he bargained, holding her gaze, "and I won't tell Whittier that the whole setup is phony—that his prize columnist is a little liar with delusions of country grandeur."

She sat up stiffly now, her entire body turned in his direction, every muscle in her taut with tension. Her voice was high. "If?"

He made himself say it without passion. With the neutrality of points bargained over a boardroom table.

"If you'll make love with me."

She looked suddenly the way he'd felt a little while ago when she'd told him she wasn't really married to Bill—as though some primitive priest had hold of her heart and was trying to rip it from her.

"Make love with you," she repeated. He remembered that he'd had to repeat everything she'd told him as though it couldn't possibly be real unless he heard himself say the words.

"Yes," he said.

"Here?" she asked. Her eyes brimmed with tears, but she sniffed and tossed her head and the tears didn't fall. "In these romantic surroundings?"

His pulse quickened and grew erratic, torn between guilt and desire.

"Has to be before the show," he replied. "In the morning we're heading for home—well, Bill's home, anyway—and the TV crew's supposed to be there.

And in the evening is the show. Tonight's the only time we have.''

She stared at him, a million things in those tear-filled velvet eyes he found difficult to look at. Pain, disappointment, disillusionment—acceptance.

She stood and began to unbutton her coat.

Instead of exhilaration, he felt anger. He didn't understand it and told himself it didn't matter.

The coat unbuttoned, she slipped out of it, then spread it open on the floor as though she intended them to lie on it. She began to work on the shirt buttons down the front of her silky green top.

"I guess," she said with a quick, lifeless smile in his direction, "I should think of this as a way of finding out if you're really worth everything I risked to get to know you."

He watched her eyes as she worked on the last button, certain she was manipulating him, that she had no intention of going through with it.

"And you'd have judged my worthiness," he asked, "on my sexual prowess?"

"It's all I have to go on," she said, pulling the shirt off, revealing small but perfect breasts cupped in scraps of black lace. "The you I thought I'd gotten to know was about as real as my family." She spread her arms out gracefully in a sort of "this is me" gesture. "Now that we've tricked each other, I guess this is all we have."

She slipped her fingers into the waistband of the pants that matched her top and he leapt up to stop her, angry with himself that he couldn't go through with it, furious that, after almost three months in captivity being tied up and fed like an animal, he was still soft enough to succumb to tears in a woman's eyes.

"All right, you've made your point," he said, snatching up her shirt and putting it roughly on her. He yanked his own coat off and dropped it on her shoulders. "Lie down on your coat and go to sleep."

Liza complied, because she didn't know what else to do. She was exhausted and filled with despair as she watched him put more wood on the fire. Everything they'd shared in the past two days had convinced her that he wouldn't be able to carry out the deal. She felt fortunate and grateful that her instincts had been correct. And more determined than ever that Jeffrey James wasn't getting away from her.

With the fire set to burn for several hours, he stepped over her feet and she heard him sit down on the bench again.

She sat up and held his coat out to him. "If you aren't coming to bed," she said, "you'll need this."

"'Coming to bed?'" he repeated dryly. "Liza, we're not Darby and Joan in New Haven. You're a liar, I'm the jerk who fell for you, and we're stuck in a cabin in the woods in ten-degree weather. Don't try to get domestic on me. You can't do it, remember?"

"Even a domestic incompetent knows that body heat will keep us warm. But if you don't want to be near me, at least take your coat back."

He stretched his legs out and crossed them at the

ankles, folded his arms and stared moodily into the fire. "Please just lie down and go to sleep."

"Not unless you join me or take your coat back."

His eyes swung from the fire to her, not one muscle in his body moving. "Liza, I have spent two interminable days in your company, tortured by sweet longings and hot desire because I believed you were married. Believe me when I tell you that I can't be trusted to hold you and do nothing about that—particularly now that I know you're single."

"Then all you felt for me was physical?"

"I thought we just established that that wasn't true? No, I'm keeping my distance for fear of murdering you before you become a national success. Since I've just regained my freedom, that wouldn't be wise. Satisfying, but not wise."

Liza leaned back into the lining of her coat, Jeff's coat slung over her. Her feet were frozen.

"Fine, then. Stay there," she said, tears burning her eyes and clogging her throat. These two days had been the most wonderful and the absolute worst fortysome hours of her life. "Murder isn't a very pleasant Christmas thought, anyway. You're the only man I know who can claim to love a woman, take her on a romantic sleigh ride in the snow and discover she's available, then threaten to murder her."

"You have an interesting concept of romantic," he disputed. "Our Santa was drunk, our sleigh crashed and you turn out to be available but *nuts*."

Liza wept silently into her coat, wondering if she was doomed to perdition for ruining Christmas for everyone and for destroying what had to have been a God-given chance to share her life with Jeff James.

Hopefully, since Jeff had seen Bill and Sherrie kissing, they at least had resolved their problems. Even though Sherrie wouldn't be able to buy the inn herself, Bill might be willing to finance her.

Mr. Whittier would be disappointed about the sudden disappearance of his ratings-making guest, but he had many connections and opportunities, and he would recover.

She was the one whose future looked bleak. She'd lost everything. The career, the opportunity and the man.

Without warning, Liza felt her upper body lifted off her coat and an arm slipped under her. At the same moment another arm came around her waist and pulled her into the curve of Jeff's body. He readjusted his coat over them and settled her so that she rested her head on his upper arm.

"You say one word," he warned, "and I won't stay. Just be quiet and go to sleep."

Jeff was surprised when she complied. He closed his eyes and tried to turn off all sensory observation—to ignore her fragrant hair under his nose, the curve of the underside of her breasts just above his arm, her bottom pressed against that part of him that yearned painfully for her. He was just beginning to think he might make it through the long hours ahead when she ran the sole of her foot against his shin.

The fabric of his slacks and her stockings lay between her skin and his, but he still found the touch erotic.

"What are you doing?" he asked in the most discouraging tone he could muster.

"My feet are frozen," she whispered. "I'm sorry. I can't tuck them high enough to get them under the coat."

He sighed, resigned to his fate. This night would be worse than anything he'd faced in captivity. "All right. Put them on me, but stop *moving*."

She put her feet against him without hesitation.

He gasped against the frigid feel of them, even through the fabric of his slacks.

"Have you no circulation below the knees?" he grumbled.

"Apparently not," she said with a dignity that belied their circumstances. "I'm trying to not even think about anything below the waist."

He raised his head to look down at her face resting on his arm. "That's suggestive. I thought you didn't *want* to make love with me."

She blew air scornfully. "You really *aren't* as intelligent as you claimed, are you? Go to sleep."

JEFF AWOKE to a thunderous banging on the cabin door. The fire still flickered, but the room was dark and frigid.

"Jeff?" a voice called between thumps. "Liza! Are you in there?"

Liza lifted her head sleepily and Jeff eased his

cramped arm out from under her. "What…is it?" she asked.

He got to his knees and pulled her to a sitting position. "Rescue," he said, recognizing Bill's voice in the shouts. "Come on, get up. Get your coat on."

Jeff jammed his arms into his own coat, then helped her with hers.

"Are you sure?" she asked, a reluctant note in her voice. "How did they find us?"

"The smoking chimney, I imagine," he said, lifting her to her feet. He eased her onto the bench, then went to the door.

Two policemen burst into the room, along with Bill and Whittier.

Bill took Jeff by the shoulders. "Thank God," he said with obvious sincerity, then spotted Liza and ran to her. He took her in his arms, the gesture genuine, Jeff was sure, and not simply for Whittier's benefit.

But Whittier smiled as he watched them, apparently taking Bill's relief at finding Liza safe as a husband's loving gratitude. Then Whittier clapped Jeff on the shoulder. "Seems you're a hero a second time."

Jeff laughed lightly. "But *you're* rescuing *us,*" he observed.

"But you protected Kowalski, found shelter, kept Liza safe."

"Kowalski?"

"The sleigh driver. His people found him a couple of hours ago. It was obvious you'd taken the horse, but when you didn't show up in town, we all went a little crazy. Where is the horse?"

Jeff pointed in the direction of the barn.

One police officer went back to the car and the other went to the barn.

"I made him turn the wrong way when we got to the road," Liza said as she and Bill joined them. "If we'd gone the way he wanted, we'd have been back at the dance before it ended."

The dance. Bill's eyes met Jeff's, a trace of grudging amusement in their depths. Jeff guessed that when Bill had taken Liza into his arms by the fireplace she'd used the opportunity to explain that the secret was out—at least partially. And that this eventful night was all the result of Jeff's misunderstanding of the kiss between Bill and Sherrie.

"The two of you picked a strange time to sight-see," Whittier observed.

Jeff saw the resignation on Liza's face, the firm grip Bill took on her shoulder as they waited to be exposed as frauds.

"I'd been telling Liza," Jeff said, "how the dry, desert landscape of Lebanon had gotten to me. She'd noticed the sleigh rides and thought I'd enjoy a drive in the snow as a sort of welcome home." He shrugged. "It was supposed to last half an hour. You know what they say about the plans of mice and men."

Liza and Bill looked at each other in surprise, then at him. He looked away.

Whittier laughed. "They also say that all's well that ends well. Come on. Let's get you two home. It's just after three. The film crew's due at nine and they'll be pretty noisy, so if you're going to get any sleep in, it'll have to be soon.''

Jeff pointed to the fireplace. "You go ahead. I'll just make sure the fire's out.''

"Hurry up," Bill advised. "We've got a thermos of coffee in the car, and Sherrie sent along some muffins.''

Jeff hunkered down in front of the fireplace, spread out the dying coals of the fire and turned them to put them out. He stared into the now-dark hole and remembered what it had been like when the fire had burned brightly, when Liza had been asleep in his arms, trustingly content despite his annoyance with her and the harsh deal he'd tried to make and been unable to carry through.

What now?

He had to admit he hadn't a clue.

He braced his hands on his knees and pushed himself to his feet, thinking that he was going to miss this little cabin.

Cold air rushed in through the open door and he hurried toward it. A cup of coffee was going to taste like heaven.

Liza stood in the doorway, blocking his exit. Bill, Whittier and one of the policemen were in the car, waiting for them.

The other officer had mounted the horse and had already started up the road.

"What?" Jeff asked.

She'd pulled her hood up and her hands were

jammed in her pockets. She looked pale and tired. "You didn't tell," she observed.

"Yet," he said, impatient with her need to make a point of the fact. "I'm looking forward to torturing you all day long with the possibility that I might spill it all at any moment."

He saw her resist the impulse to smile. Now he was irritated as well as impatient.

"Then I'd like to make a deal with you," she offered.

Déjà vu, he thought, only now the *vu* was on the other foot—so to speak.

"And what are the terms?" he asked.

"If you'll remain silent about what you know until after the show," she bargained, "I'll make love with you when it's over."

His heart's desire neatly wrapped and handed to him. Only a curious evolution had taken place in him overnight, and now that was no longer enough.

Also, this woman had driven him insane with wanting her while letting him think she was Bill's wife, and she still thought she could call the tune.

"No, thanks," he said, and tried to push past her.

She looked up at him, clearly stunned, and remained in the doorway.

"What do you mean?" she demanded in a whisper.

"I mean no," he said, putting a hand to her shoulder and pushing her gently backward until he could close the door. "It's the opposite of yes. A negative, a refusal, a denial."

She remained with her back to the car. "I understand the word," she said, her pallor turning to a flush, "but why are you using it? Last night you proposed the same deal to me!"

"Last night it was in my favor," he said, taking her arm and smiling so that the observers in the car would think it was a simple conversation being shared by two people who'd been through a lot together. "Today it's in yours, and after the way you lied to me and used me, I'm not in the mood to give you any advantages."

He walked her around the back of the car to the other side.

"You mean," she asked stiffly, "that you would only make love to me if *you* had the advantage in the encounter?"

"Of course, if it was part of a deal."

She reached for the door handle at the same moment that he did, stopping him from opening the car door. "And if it wasn't part of a deal?"

"That would be another story," he said. "But that wasn't what you offered me. Get in."

They were home in twenty minutes. Sherrie burst into tears and hugged Liza, then Jeff, then drew them both to the fire.

"We were frantic!" she exclaimed, hugging Liza again. "Then when they found the sleigh driver and there was no sign of the two of you…!"

Whittier patted Liza's shoulder. "Apparently our little country girl has a very poor sense of direction. Bill says she's always been like that."

Sherrie nodded. "She gets lost in office buildings,

department stores, shopping malls. Theme parks are out of the question.''

Whittier laughed, then hugged Liza awkwardly. ''I guess that's why she prefers the country. She's just a sweet, uncomplicated hearth mother.''

Sherrie coughed. ''Yes, that's our Liza.'' She turned Whittier toward the stairs. ''Why don't you go up to bed, Mr. Whittier? I'm going to try to warm up these two with some soup. You'll have to be fresh when the film crew arrives.''

''Right. If you're sure there's nothing I can do.''

''Nothing. Thank you.''

''Well.'' Whittier sketched a wave at Liza, then at Jeff. ''See you in the morning. Tomorrow's our big night. Have to admit you two had me a little worried there.''

''No need to worry, Mr. Whittier,'' Liza said with a challenging stare in Jeff's direction. ''The show will be great.''

''I know it will.'' He waved again from the railing as he turned down the upstairs corridor to his room.

Sherrie took Liza's coat from her, wrapped a blanket around her shoulders and pushed her into one of the red wing chairs pulled up to the fire. ''Just relax, and I'll get that soup. Jeff, give me your coat.''

Bill helped him off with it, then took Liza's coat from Sherrie and went to the hall closet with them.

Liza eased her stiff and frozen feet out of her pumps and held them up to the flames with a wince of pain. ''I'm never wearing anything but tennies again," she declared, gingerly wriggling her toes. "Or maybe boots."

"Well, that's what you get for haring off in a sleigh in a snowstorm!" Sherrie barked.

Jeff guessed that residual stress was making itself felt now that her sister was safe and sound in front of a fire. Then she seemed to realize there was no reason to shout and cleared her throat self-consciously.

"I'm sorry," she said. "It's been a very long six hours."

She cleared her throat again, selected the poker from the fireplace tools and jabbed at the fire unnecessarily.

"I know what you saw behind the coatrack upset you, Jeff," she said as though she'd been rehearsing the little speech the entire six hours, "but there's a perfectly reasonable explanation, which we'd have given you if you hadn't jumped to conclusions and taken off like some rabid reindeer and almost killed my sister!"

"Sherrie!" Liza said firmly. "The sleigh driver is the one who almost killed both of us, and I'm the one who got us lost."

"And reindeer pull the sleigh," Bill said as he rejoined them. "They don't usually ride in the front."

Sherrie turned on him, apparently indignant at his attempt at humor. Jeff intervened, realizing that he could really like Bill now that he wasn't married to Liza.

"And what is the explanation for that kiss?" Jeff asked.

Sherrie, unaware that he knew the truth, squared her shoulders and tried to give it. She looked right into his eyes. "Mistletoe," she said.

Liza closed her eyes. Bill put a hand over his.

"Mistletoe," Jeff repeated.

"Yes." He admired the way she ignored her sister's and Bill's reactions and forged on. "Liza's doing a segment on it for the show and we were...sort of...rehearsing it."

"Really."

"Yes. It was worshiped by the Druids, you know. They passed it among their members for good luck in the New Year."

"I see." It took great effort to keep a straight face. "And there was mistletoe above the coatrack?"

She ignored his question. "Frigga, the Scandinavian goddess, was the first to stand under it, waiting for a kiss."

"From her husband, Odin, the god of the Norse?"

She studied his face with sudden distrust. "Yes," she replied.

"And was that in a coatroom, do you think?"

She opened her mouth to respond, but Liza cut her off. "Relax, Sherrie, he knows. I told him everything. He's just amusing himself with you." Liza gave him a scolding glance. "He likes to do that."

Sherrie turned on him with a glower. "Jeff, I warn you that my sense of humor is about this big right now." She held her thumb and forefinger about a centimeter apart. "So I wouldn't trifle with me, if I were you. Particularly if you're hoping for soup *in* you and not *on* you."

"I apologize for your stressful night," he said, refusing to appear repentant. "But I left the dance with Liza because I thought you and Bill were playing Madame Bovary rather than Norse mythology. Considering you'd all lied to me about who was who, I think you can be a little more tolerant of what's happened, and maybe even rethink who's to blame."

"Don't yell at them," Liza said defensively, getting to her feet. "They're involved because I talked them into it. The blame is entirely mine."

"We should all stop yelling," Bill said quietly, trying to push her back into her chair, "or Whittier's going to be down here wanting to know what's going on."

Liza pushed his hands away. "You're not playing my husband anymore, Bill McBride, so don't try to tell me what to do. And the next time you take on the role of husband, you might remember that it generally doesn't include games of kissy-face behind the trench coats with another woman!"

"Don't blame him," Sherrie began. "You—"

Liza rounded on her. "And you! When you hire on to be somebody's assistant, and that somebody is supposed to have a husband, it would help the scenario a lot if you weren't giving the husband smoldering looks!"

"I never..." Sherrie began to deny.

"Yes, you did," Jeff disputed. "All the time.

That's what led me to believe the two of you were fooling around on Liza in the first place."

"That's because she loves me," Bill said with the easy matter-of-factness Jeff had come to admire. "But she's afraid to admit it, so she has to say it with looks instead of with words. So if anyone's to blame for tonight, it's her."

"Oh, really." Sherrie turned on him. "Who cornered who in the coatroom?"

"Who didn't resist?"

"All right, I've had it with all of you!" Liza fought her way out of the blanket around her shoulders and glared at each of them, one at a time. "All our lives are going to hell and instead of doing anything constructive about it, all you can do is shout at one another. Well, it's going to be my face in front of the camera tomorrow, so I'm going to bed!"

She headed off toward the stairs, took three steps and fell flat on her face.

Chapter Ten

Liza lay with her nose in Bill's colorful Oriental carpet and thought with resignation, *Well, why not? Why should the simple act of putting one foot in front of the other go any better than the rest of the night had gone?*

"She's fainted!" she heard Sherrie cry. "She's never fainted before! She's the strongest, toughest..."

Liza lost track of her sister's ramblings as strong male hands turned her over. Jeff and Bill knelt over her, Jeff looking worried, Bill suddenly very professional.

"I didn't faint," she said, trying to push Bill's hands away as he felt for a pulse at her throat.

Jeff caught her hands and held them immobile so that Bill could work.

"I didn't..." she began again.

"Shh!" Bill ordered sharply.

She remained quiet for a moment while Bill checked her pulse, looked into her eyes, felt her cheek and forehead.

"She didn't faint," he announced finally.

"Then what happened?" Jeff asked.

"Would anyone like to ask me?" Liza pushed Jeff's hands away and sat up. "My feet," she volunteered when no one asked, "are so cold they wouldn't work. That's all. I'm sure if I try one more time..."

That option was taken from her when Jeff lifted her into his arms. "I'll take her upstairs and put her under the covers," he said to Sherrie.

"Good. I'll bring your soup up. Bill, would you move Betsy into my room for tonight? Certainly Whittier wouldn't question that, considering what Liza's been through tonight."

"Right."

Liza wanted to protest that she would be fine, that she was perfectly capable of walking on her own, but it was deliciously comfortable in Jeff's arms, and being carried upstairs reminded her of the other time he'd done it, when he'd looked at her with such longing she'd thought her heart would break.

This time his touch was more proprietary but less tender. It would be a long time before he forgave her for lying to him—if he ever did at all.

He placed her on the bed in Bill's room while Bill wheeled Betsy and her crib out and down the hall. Liza braced herself on her heels and elbows while Jeff worked the blankets and comforter out from under her, then brought them up as far as her waist.

"What do you wear to bed?" he asked, going to the dresser.

"Flannel nightshirt," she said, pointing to the bottom drawer.

He came back to the bed with the red-and-blue-plaid nightshirt with a lace ruffle around the collar. He held it up and grinned. "I see you've chosen function over glamour. Women don't usually do that."

"I guess I knew," she said, "that I was going to get frostbitten in the Connecticut countryside with a man determined to keep his cool."

"If I lose my cool," he reminded her, "your career goes up in flames, along with your editor's job and Sherrie's inn. Put that on. I've got just the thing to complete the look."

Liza scrambled out of her clothes and into the nightie while he left the room. When he returned, she sat primly against the pillows, the blankets pulled up to her chest, her clothes in a tidy pile on the chair.

"Boot socks," he said, holding up a large wad of gray wool with red toes and ribbing. "Stick your feet out the side."

He sat on the edge of the bed, took her feet onto his lap and put the thick socks on her. "God. They're like chunks of polar ice cap." He rubbed one foot, then the other, then went back to the first to manipulate her toes, then worked on the second foot.

Liza watched him and told herself bracingly that he didn't act like a man who didn't care. His touch was vigorous but gentle, possessive but respectful.

Sherrie came up with a tray bearing mugs of soup and chunks of bread. She placed it on Liza's bedside table. "Will you stay and keep an eye on her?" she asked Jeff, her expression completely guileless. "I want to check on the children and get a few things ready for tomorrow. I couldn't concentrate while the two of you were lost."

"Ah...sure."

He didn't look like a man who didn't care, Liza thought dispiritedly, but he didn't look like a man who was ready to die for her, either. Not that she'd want him to.

"Good." Sherrie smiled. "I'll close the door so that if Whittier wanders around, he won't see you in here and wonder."

Liza tossed the blankets back on the other side of the bed and patted the flowered sheet. "Sit down here and eat your soup. I'm wearing too much to be any kind of a threat to you."

He walked around to the empty side of the bed and sat against the pillows, pulled his shoes off and stretched his legs out under the covers. She handed him a mug of soup.

"Thank you," he said, taking it from her. "You know, you underestimate yourself if you think clothes diminish your...*threat*." He repeated her word with emphasis, as though he disagreed with the choice of it. "Or that they would stop me anyway if I succumbed to it."

She blew lightly into the steaming cup of beef barley. "There's no chance of that happening," she said, deliberately trying to bait him.

He nodded. "There isn't, but why do you think so?"

"Because you're a man who never takes action without understanding all the details," she said, then took a cautious sip. She chewed and swallowed, the hot, homey flavors of beef and grain somehow beginning to restore her sense of purpose. She hadn't Sherrie's cooking skills or her nimble fingers with crafts, but the *Wonder Woman* column had come out of her imagination, out of her own hopes and dreams. "You told me so yourself. And you can never know another person—a lover—like you know the rules of mathematics and science. You can't build a woman like you build a bridge or a road."

He gave her a dry look. "Big talk from a woman who doesn't know east from west. And usually when you go for the details, you can assess whether something is right or wrong, if it's true or a lie. You artistic types who claim to opt for the bigger picture seem to get a little foggy on those issues."

"I still maintain that my intentions were good."

"Attila the Hun probably thought his intentions were good, but I doubt that the Roman Empire had any sympathy with that."

"You don't think," she asked in exasperation, "that comparing me to Attila the Hun is a little bit of a stretch? See if I ever invite you for Christmas again."

"If you did, I gather I'd be spending it in some Manhattan high-rise. Where did this thirst for country living come from, anyway?"

She took a deep sip of soup and struggled against the sleepiness beginning to overtake her. "Too many years of big-city living, I guess. My father died when Sherrie and I were small, and my mother had to give up the house and move us into an apartment. City living has its advantages, but I always longed for trees and lawns and maybe the sound of water.''

"Why," he asked, "after your considerable success, are you still living in Manhattan?"

"Student loans, savings that were depleted when I was between jobs, the proximity to work." She put her mug aside and leaned back into the pillows. "And I'm lacking someone to share the country with."

"You're telling me there are no men in your life?"

She turned restlessly onto her side. He held his cup up to avoid a spill. "Not the right one," she said into her pillow.

"What defines the right one?"

She turned onto her other side, toward him, a pleat between her eyebrows. His soup sloshed and he gave up on it, putting it on the bedside table.

"Niceness," she said drowsily, "tolerance." She yawned. "A sense of hope and..." She turned onto her back. "A love of...children and...country life."

She stirred restlessly and sat up, her eyes barely open. "Something hurts," she complained, trying to reach over her shoulder to her back.

He looked down at her pillows and saw nothing, then ran a hand over the flannel down the middle of her back and encountered the unyielding metal of three small hooks.

"You left your bra on," he said. He patted her flannel-covered hip. "Lift up and I'll unhook you."

She complied and he reached under the flannel, felt the silky warmth of her back and the closure of the bra. He unhooked it, tugged gently, and found himself holding the length of black lace he'd caught a glimpse of earlier when she'd pretended to comply with his terms of the deal. He tossed it toward the rest of her things.

Liza turned, her eyes closing, and fell into his arms. As clearly as though he could see them, her small, warm breasts pressed into his chest, making him feel as though they'd branded him.

And just as quickly, she was asleep.

Twice in one night, he thought, trying to deal with her soft suppleness against his severely deprived body. God was toying with him.

He slept and dreamed of freedom. He drove a sleigh through Beirut, Father Chabot seated beside him, and no one followed them or tried to stop them. The sleigh was drawn by a single reindeer with a red nose.

The countryside went by in a rush and when he looked again he recognized the trees, the rolling hills, the classic church steeples and old homes of rural Connecticut.

Then their path was blocked by an angel with long blond hair and bright brown eyes. She was a classic tree-topper angel in a flowing white robe, with wings and a halo. The only discordant note in her appearance was a gingham apron.

He reached for her and she disappeared.

He awoke with a start to the flimsy gray light of

dawn. Despite the dream curiously braided with old and new memories, he knew precisely where he was.

His only confusion was that Liza no longer lay in his arms, but sat up beside him as though she'd been watching him while he slept. In the frail light she had the misty look of the angel in his dream. His left arm was extended, and her fingers were entangled in his.

"What happened?" he asked.

She shrugged a shoulder under the flannel, giving him a smile that warmed him to the marrow of his bones. "You were dreaming," she said. "And you reached out for me." She squeezed his hand. "So I caught you."

He used that hand to pull her into his arms. She came eagerly, all warmth and softness and whispered endearments.

"Jeff, I knew it the first time I saw you," she said. "I knew it. And I understand why you think I'm a liar and a phony, but I…"

He knew disputing her claims would take time and effort—effort better spent on other things—so he opted for expedience and simply kissed her into silence.

Her supple mouth was everything he'd imagined it would be when he'd seen her on television last Christmas and been so fascinated by her lips that he'd watched her form every word.

Now they responded to him artfully, ardently, and her body leaned into his and wrapped around it with an impassioned tenderness that was new in his experience. It occurred to him that if the world stopped now, he would die a happy man.

He ran a hand under her nightshirt, feeling the silk of her in his palm as he stroked over the curve of her hip and up into the hollow of her waist.

She sighed against his mouth and tried to reach under his shirt, but he'd gone to sleep last night still fully dressed.

He braced up on an elbow and pulled at his shirt, Liza helping him. But their movements were interrupted by a light rap on the door.

"Oh no!" Liza gasped.

Frustration mingled with fear of Liza being discovered in bed with her houseguest galvanized Jeff into action. He leapt out of the bed and hid behind the louvered doors where Bill's bed was.

"Yes?" Liza asked calmly.

The bedroom door opened and closed quickly. "They're here!" It was Sherrie's voice, high and frantic. "They weren't due until nine, but they're here now!"

Jeff opened the closet door to see her run across the room to the window, Liza right behind her. He looked down over their shoulders to see cars and trucks streaming up the driveway. The film crew had arrived.

"Whittier'll be waking up any minute!" Sherrie whispered, looking at Liza apologetically. "I'm sorry. I should have awakened Jeff last night, but you were sleeping so comfortably against him and it had been such a rotten night."

"Mmm," Liza said. "And the fact that that meant Bill had to stay with you didn't hurt, either."

Sherrie smiled widely. "We're getting married New Year's Eve."

"All *right!*" Liza wrapped her arms around Sherrie and hugged her tightly. "I'm so happy. It's about time!" Then she held her away from her and added with mock severity, "But none of those molten looks until *after* the show."

"Right."

Jeff was surprised when Sherrie caught his arm and led him toward the door with a grateful smile. "Thank you," she said.

He raised an eyebrow. "For what?"

"Lots of things," she replied. "Too much to go into now." Then she pushed him behind the door, pulled it open cautiously and peered around it.

"Sherrie!" Whittier's voice boomed. "The film crew's here early!"

Jeff held himself flatly to the wall. From the bed, Liza puckered her lips and made a kissing motion at him.

"I know," Sherrie said to Whittier. "I heard them and came in to wake Liza."

"How is she after last night?" Whittier asked. Jeff guessed his concern was as much for the show as for his columnist. "The crew's going to want to shoot her and Bill and the outside of the house."

"She's just about to wake herself up with a shower," Sherrie said.

"Can I say good morning?"

Jeff closed his eyes, certain discovery was imminent.

"I'll give her the message, Mr. Whittier," Sherrie said. "She's not decent. If you'll go downstairs, the coffee should be on and I'll be there in a few minutes to make you my special French toast."

"Special?" he asked interestedly.

"I make it with sliced cinnamon rolls."

"Ooh! I'll even set the table."

"Thank you. I won't be long." Sherrie closed the door, then leaned back against it with a strangled little gasp. "Liza," she said, "when this is over I may kill you."

Liza sat up with a broad grin. "When this is over you'll be too busy running the inn and catering to your husband and children."

"Yeah, well, until the show's over, they're *your* husband and children, so get moving. You heard Whittier." Sherrie opened the door several inches, peered out, then caught Jeff's arm and pulled him with her out into the hall. Then she pushed him toward his room. She blew him a kiss as she headed for her room and a bawling Betsy.

Liza showered, put on a blue sweater over blue leggings and pulled on a pair of high black boots.

She was stunned by how calm she felt when she walked downstairs to find Bill's house filled to capacity with people and equipment. The boys were rubbernecking as a cameraman set up near the Christmas tree.

A young woman wearing earphones had Betsy in

one arm and was supervising the setting up of lights behind the camera.

They were like a friendly group of aliens, Liza decided as she exchanged greetings, waves and smiles with them on her way to the kitchen. Looking at their headgear, their otherworldly equipment, and listening to their strange vocabulary, she felt the way Richard Dreyfuss must have felt at the end of *Close Encounters of the Third Kind* when he cleared the top of the ramp and entered the spaceship.

She found Whittier at the table with a handsome fair-haired man she guessed to be about Jeff's age.

"Liza, I'd like you to meet, Chris Page, our producer," Whittier said, standing to pull out a chair for her. "Chris, this is Liza De Lane."

Chris stood also, his smile reserved and professional. "Pleased to meet you, Miss De Lane. We have a big day ahead of us."

She reached across the table to shake his hand. "Then you'd better call me Liza."

"And you'd better have seconds on the French toast." Sherrie refilled his plate and added another piece to Whittier's.

Bill shouldered the back door open and walked into the kitchen with an armload of wood. He dropped it in the wood bin, then pulled off his gloves and jacket and came around the table to kiss Liza's cheek, apparently prepared to be onstage for the day.

"Good morning," he said. "I'm surprised you're up so early. How do you feel?"

"Mr. Whittier was telling me about your accident

last night,'' Chris Page sympathized, then smiled. ''I understand we almost had to replace you with back-to-back 'Lucy' reruns.''

Liza laughed as Sherrie brought her a plate of French toast. ''You may think that's happened anyway. Sherrie and I in action are a lot like Lucy and Ethel.''

''The only resemblance is that they, too, are brilliant,'' Whittier said magnanimously. ''Ah. Here's Jeff James.''

Jeff walked into the room and Liza devoured the sight of him in jeans and an oatmeal-colored pullover. Then she remembered that she couldn't let what he meant to her show on her face—at least, not until after the filming.

She put a hand on his arm as Chris stood again to be introduced. She watched Jeff shake hands with the producer, laugh about last night's experience and say with a grin in her direction, ''I'll be able to tell my grandchildren that I spent the night in a remote little cabin with Liza De Lane. I'll leave out the part about her being married to someone else and that all we did was sit on a bench in front of a fire and swap childhood stories.''

''Mr. Whittier insists that you saved her life,'' Chris said, then waited hopefully for confirmation.

Jeff shook his head. ''I don't think we were ever in danger of death. Of frostbitten toes, maybe. I am in danger of losing my heart to this family, though.'' Jeff spread both arms to indicate their surroundings. ''Can you imagine a better place to spend Christmas?

I'm considering trying to talk the city fathers into some major engineering project so I can stay here.''

Liza heard those words with a little thrill of excitement. Was there a chance this would all work out after all? Could she pull this off? Do the show, and explain later when she married Jeff that she'd just stood in for her sister as Bill's wife and the children's mother because Sherrie was too shy to appear before a camera?

Had she any right to hope that it could be that simple?

No. Of course not. And that was proven a moment later when the doorbell rang.

Liza stood and pushed Bill into her chair. "You're the one who's been hauling wood—you should eat first." She kissed the top of his head for effect. "I'll get the door."

She sidestepped cameras, lighting and sound equipment and members of the crew, and stepped over wires and cables as she carefully picked her way to the door.

She pulled it open and looked into the face of a gorgeous, dark-haired woman in a white wool coat with a fox fur collar. Liza studied it lustfully. She was as opposed to the wearing of fur as any animal activist, and she didn't mourn the loss of mink or sable in fashion, but there was something about the feel of fox against a woman's throat that made her wish it could be replicated by a manufacturer.

The woman gave her a bright smile. Her hair was worn in an elegant knot, her seductively slanted hazel eyes and her beautifully creamy skin were elegantly made up, and she had a mole at the corner of wine-colored lips.

Liza wondered absently if the producer had hired a model or an actress to fill in.

The woman gasped with what seemed to be pleasure, then wrapped her arms around Liza. "You're her!" she said in a husky voice. "You're Liza De Lane! I can't believe this. I'm actually on Liza De Lane's doorstep!"

Still confused about who she was, Liza drew her inside and closed the door. "I'm sorry, I—" she began, but the woman cut her off with a glance beyond Liza's head.

"My goodness! Will you look at that! The big time. National television. I'm *so* excited for you! You just *burst* right out of that little cable show."

"Thank you. I'm af—"

"Who's producing this for you? Is it Chris Page? He's the best, you know. Martha Stewart has him written into all her contracts."

"Yes," Liza replied, feeling a little as though she'd been caught in a tornado. "Are you—?"

"Is he here?" the woman interrupted again. "Please tell me he's here!"

"Chris Page? Yes, he's in…" She swept a hand toward the kitchen.

"No!" The woman's right hand, with a large diamond on the third finger, swept the air. "Not Chris Page. Although I can't believe *he's* here, too! I mean Jeffrey James."

"Oh. Yes, he's here also." Liza led her toward the kitchen, pointing to the wires and cables and cautioning her to watch her step. "Jeff," she said when they'd reached the long table where the men were dividing up the morning paper, "there's an admirer here to see—"

She got no further. The woman squealed, Jeff got to his feet with a wide smile, opened his arms, and the woman ran into them. She flung her fox-trimmed arms around him and planted a kiss on his lips that had the other three men staring at Jeff in wistful jealousy. The black leather pump on her left foot rose with the graceful little backward kick of her leg as the kiss went on and on.

They finally drew apart and the woman's voice, low and husky, said heavily, "Jeffrey. Darling."

"Sylvia." His voice was lost in her fox collar as she brought him close to her again.

Chapter Eleven

Liza stood by, smiling, while Jeff introduced Sylvia to the group. But her mouth ached from the effort and her heart ached with the memory of Jeff's obvious delight at Sylvia's arrival, and Sylvia's clear adoration of him. Liza wouldn't even allow herself to think about the kiss.

"I apologize for intruding upon your Christmas celebration," Sylvia said with a smile for every male face at the table. She wasn't manipulative, Liza noted fairly, just the kind of woman who found men endlessly interesting, and knew precisely how to capture *their* interest.

She pushed Jeff into his chair, shed her coat with a graceful toss of her shoulders and settled herself in his lap. "Jeff and I were together for a year before he went to Lebanon." She spoke to the assembled group but her eyes kept returning to Jeff's gaze. A pleat of regret appeared between her beautifully arched eyebrows. "Then we quarreled, I thought loving someone else would be easier than loving Jeff and…" She smiled wistfully. "But love is never easy,

I guess. Then Jeff's escape was all over the news and I *had* to see for myself that he was all right.''

''Where's… What was his name?'' Jeff asked.

''Bobby Hickock.'' She shrugged. ''Still in Dallas, I expect. What I'm more interested in is…where are *we?*''

Chris cleared his throat to claim their attention. ''I'm thinking,'' he said, ''that this would make a good interview to put in toward the end of the show. It's a great romantic element, you know? The hero's former love hears about his plight and rushes home to find him and spend Christmas with him. You two have a problem with sitting in front of the Christmas tree and telling your story?''

''That'd be perfect!'' Whittier said with a thump of his fist on the table. The crockery shook and he put both hands down to stop it. ''That's the kind of thing that drives the viewers wild!''

Jeff turned to Liza.

Now she let herself remember the kiss he and Sylvia had shared and made an instant decision. This day was about scores of people putting in very expensive time to produce a television special that would make Whittier happy, boost Edie's career, provide Sherrie with the capital to buy the inn and give Liza the national exposure any popular columnist would be thrilled to get.

It was about professionalism, not pipe dreams.

''That'd be a lovely touch,'' she said, not sure where the words or the cheerful tone came from. She felt like the bottom of a swamp. ''You go ahead and do that. You'll have to excuse me, though. Sherrie and I have a million things to get ready."

"Sure." Chris accepted that with unflattering ease, then talked over a few details with Whittier as they all headed for the living room.

Jeff stopped in the doorway to give Liza one dark, lingering look.

She met it with a blank smile and a shooing motion of both hands. "Go," she said. "It's a wonderful idea. Really."

To everyone else it sounded as though she meant the segment was a wonderful idea, when in truth she was telling him not to worry about what had passed between them. It had been the result of the schmaltzy emotion of Christmastime and two people who'd found each other on television and discovered that in person, other people and things had claim on their lives.

"What do you mean it's a wonderful idea?" Sherrie asked under her breath, dragging her into a corner of the kitchen where they couldn't be seen from the living room. "You love him, remember?"

"Well, he seems to love *her*," she said, trying to free herself from her sister's grip. Sherrie held on.

"He barely got a word in!"

"Yes, he did," Liza disputed. "He said 'Sylvia.' With real feeling."

"That was shock."

"It was passion."

"You're an idiot." A technician walked into the kitchen in search of a glass of water, and Sherrie handed him a stack of paper cups and a pitcher of water filled with lemon slices. "I second-guessed you," she said with a smile. "Please don't electrocute anyone."

The young man grinned. "There's always someone taking the fun out of everything."

The moment he was gone, Sherrie narrowed her gaze on Liza again. "He kept looking at you, waiting for you to say something."

"Yes." Liza closed her eyes. "And what would that be? No, you can't have him, he's mine? I'm really married to Bill McBride, but I'd like to keep Jeff James on the side, so keep your mitts off him?"

Sherrie put a hand to her forehead. Liza remembered that impatient gesture from many times in their childhood when she'd driven her big sister to the edge. "I'm sure if your heart had been in it, you could have come up with something. You've extricated yourself and the rest of us from a few sticky situations over the last few days. You're just jealous, so you're retreating rather than putting up a fight."

Liza glowered at her. "I'm putting up a fight for my job and your inn! Would you please give me something to do," she added in a whisper, "so that I look like I know what I'm writing about?"

When Chris returned to the kitchen twenty minutes later, Liza was at the kitchen table shelling chestnuts with a hammer.

"Amazing," he observed, watching her swing the hammer and not only crack the shell but pulverize the nut as well. "You'd think with the new kitchen technology someone would come up with a better way to shell nuts.''

Sherrie came to stand over her, wiping her hands on a towel. "She prefers old-fashioned methods. Less...bruising to the nut." Then she noticed the state of the chestnut Liza had just cracked and added with a diplomatic smile, "Well, usually. Sometimes she just puts too much enthusiasm into things."

"If you can spare her," Chris said, "I'll put another camera on following Bill and Liza and the children around for an hour or so. Then I promise I won't get in your way again until we're on."

Sherrie took the hammer from Liza. "Yes, you may have her. And I'd like to say that you don't have to bring her back, but unfortunately, she's the star of everything around here."

Betsy sat contentedly in Liza's arms and Travis and Davey flanked Bill as the camera filmed them in front of the classic home.

"Welcome to the McBride home," Liza said, slipping easily into her public persona. She wondered about the comfort she found in speaking to the camera when she'd done it only once before, on the cable show, which had had a much smaller audience.

Then she realized that today, anyway, its appeal was that she didn't have to be herself. She wasn't the woman everyone was annoyed with because she'd completely upset their lives. She wasn't the woman with the dream snapped in two by the arrival of the woman Jeff had always talked about with affection and respect. She wasn't the woman who would have to explain to Whittier after the holidays that she wasn't sure she could do this anymore.

At this moment she was who she claimed to be—Liza De Lane, expert on everything festive and domestic.

She tucked her arm in Bill's. "I'm Liza De Lane, and this is my husband, Bill McBride. He's a pediatrician, which comes in very handy with three accident-prone children." She pointed to Travis. "This is Travis, a ten-year-old baseball star with an interest in space and girls."

"Yuk!" Travis declared, sticking out his tongue. Sherrie would have been horrified to see that, but the audience, Liza knew, would love it.

"Davey is eight," Liza went on, "is a very good student and is probably the reason AOL is having trouble servicing their *other* Internet clients."

Davey waved shyly at the camera.

"And this is Betsy. She just had her first birthday. Wave to our friends, Betsy."

To Liza's amazement, Betsy waved.

The camera crew followed Liza and Bill and the children around while Liza talked about the house, about the flowers that were visible in the spring, and about the deck Bill planned to build next summer. Then she handed Betsy to Bill.

"But we know that what you've really come by for," she said, connecting to the public somewhere out there, who weren't even in front of their televisions yet but with whom she'd established a rapport in her columns, "is to see how my sister and assistant,

Sherrie Blake, and I have decorated the house, and to see what we've fixed for dinner.''

She leaned intimately close to the camera and made a beckoning gesture. "So, come in and spend Christmas Eve with us. We've been waiting for you.''

"Excellent!" Chris praised. "All right. Now let's do the step-by-step on that craft angel Whittier keeps talking about.''

As the camera crew went back into the house, Liza smiled at Bill, kissed the baby's cheek and thanked the boys.

"You guys are being the best family a woman could hope for. Do you mind checking with Sherrie to see if she needs your help with anything while I film the craft segment? Then *I'll* be her slave for the rest of the day and you guys will be free to do whatever you want until we have to get ready to go on the air.''

The boys ran off. Bill lingered to give her a supportive hug. "I wouldn't jump to conclusions about Sylvia What's-her-name.''

"You saw that kiss," she said. "The conclusion jumped at *me*.''

"But the two of you—''

"Met by seeing each other on television," she said, "and since we've met I've lied to him, shocked him, gotten him lost and almost frozen. I imagine he's probably very grateful to have a sane woman back in his life. Gotta go, Bill." She blew him a kiss. "Thanks again. See you later this afternoon.''

The angel segment was intended to follow Liza's

live tour of the house and several quick hints for decorating. It was intended to allow a little breathing space in the live presentation.

Liza and Sherrie had created the angel together several months earlier, and the response from Liza's readers had been so enormous that Sherrie had drafted a pattern. The *Wonder Woman* support staff had sent out thousands.

It involved a small drawstring bag filled with fragrant herbs that served as the body of the angel. A wooden ball painted with features was glued inside the ruffled collar created by the drawstring, then topped with hair made from yarn, cotton, or angel hair. The wings were made of raffia.

"If your angel is going to sit on a tabletop," Liza explained to the camera, holding up an angel, "simply tie the raffia in a bow, attach the wings to the back of the angel's gown with a couple of stitches or hot glue and add a little sand with your herbs for weight, or place a weight in the base before you add the herbs."

She put that angel down and held up another prepared for the Christmas tree. "If you'd like to attach your angel to the tree or to a swag, loop a gold cord around the knot on the bow of her wings before attaching them. Or a hanger made of fishing line will make her look as though she's really flying."

Liza looped the fishing line on her finger and held up the angel. Then she invited the camera down to the surface of her table where she'd spread out an array of decorations for the angel's gown.

"To make your angel extraspecial, decorate her with tiny buttons, pearls, sequins, lace, baby ribbon, tiny silk flowers, or miniature charms. Or you can make her a country-style angel by giving her a sprig of mountain laurel to hold, a tiny mushroom robin, or a dried nutmeg seed.

"However you decorate her, she'll be special because you made her with your own heart and hands. And if you give her away, she'll spread your Christmas magic.

"We'll be right back after this station break to take you into the kitchen and show you what's cooking. And we've invited a very special guest to share Christmas Eve dinner with us." Liza swallowed around the lump in her throat as she read the words leading into the station break. They'd been written days ago, but now they had an impact on her she hadn't imagined then. "I'm sure you've heard on the news that Jeffrey James, the engineer from Boston who was captured by the Fatwa Jihad while working in Beirut, escaped a week ago with Père Etienne Chabot of the D'Arc Fathers. Father Chabot is home in Paris recovering from a gunshot wound sustained during their escape, and Father Chabot credits Jeffrey James with saving his life. Stay tuned and hear how he planned the escape, carried it out, then kept the injured priest alive for six long days while on the run, inching his way toward the American embassy in Damascus. Stay with us."

"Again, excellent! Thanks, guys." Chris waved off the camera crew and put a hand on Liza's shoulder.

"You're a real natural at this," he said. "I'd have guessed you've had a lot more on-air experience than one cable show. You'd better clear the decks and make some time, because after tonight you're going to be in demand."

Liza smiled and hoped he was right. After tonight she was going to need things to occupy her time. Jeff was going home with Sylvia, and Whittier was probably going to go ballistic when he learned that his country columnist's assistant was going to marry said columnist's husband. Explaining would undoubtedly result in a lot of free time.

As Chris left to check on other aspects of the preparations, Liza cleared off all the angel materials into a box, then went to check on Sherrie's progress at the other end of the kitchen.

Sherrie rubbed her forehead with the back of her hand, a cutting board covered with sliced butternut squash on the counter in front of her.

"How's it going?" Liza asked.

"Um…okay," Sherrie said. She pointed to a jar of cloves and a bowl of apricots. "If you want to peel and halve the apricots, we can get the ham ready to go in the oven. Did you get something to eat?"

Liza took a fruit and handed one to Sherrie. "This'll keep us going. Shall I get Dora in to help?"

"No, she's keeping Betsy out of harm's way. It's just me and you."

"Okay. I'm up for it. This is our flambé dish, right? Flaming squash flan, or something?"

"Boozy Butternut Flan," Sherrie corrected with a

worried glance at her. "If you're going to talk about this stuff in front of millions of people, you should know what it's called. Where's Whittier?"

Liza hooked a thumb over her shoulder. "Last I saw, he was overseeing the interview with Jeff and Sylvia."

"Is that still going on?"

"No, it's over." The reply was made in a deep male voice.

Liza's arm was taken in a biting grip and she was turned to face Jeff. Anger simmered in him, firming the lines of his jaw, darkening his eyes. He turned to Sherrie and said politely, "Excuse us. I'm going to borrow her for a minute."

"Jeff, Sherrie and I have a million details…" Liza began to protest, but Sherrie said airily, "Sure. She tends to get in my way, anyway."

"Oh, really. Well, maybe you'd like to…" Liza stopped because Sherrie was measuring brown sugar into a pan and not listening, and Jeff had already dragged her toward the door.

She glared up at him as he took her coat off a peg and handed it to her.

"Look, if Whittier sees you with your hands on me," she began to warn him, "he'll—"

"Whittier's being filmed even as we speak," he said stiffly, "telling the story of how *Wonder Woman Magazine* owns the genius of the country's cozy-living guru." Then he opened the back door and pushed her out into the cold. "I saw Chris Page with his hands on you," he said, taking her arm and pulling her with him as he headed off across the backyard and toward the stone wall. "You didn't seem to be concerned with what Whittier would think about that."

She stopped to look up at him in exasperation. "Chris Page did *not*—"

"Oh, be quiet," he said, tugging her along with him. "I didn't come out here to talk about him, anyway."

Liza had no choice but to hurry along with him, snow crunching under their feet as he continued the forced march.

He stopped at the wall and turned to face her.

"This is not a convenient time for me, Jeff," she said, hiding her heartbreak under a guise of boredom. She drew her hands up into the sleeves of her coat. "What is your problem, and what do you expect me to do about it hours before my first national television show?"

"I don't give a rip if it's convenient or not, Liza," he returned with a mildness she knew better than to trust. Every other signal from his body suggested trouble. "You messed with my life at a time that was very inconvenient for me, but that didn't seem to bother you."

"I didn't mess with your life," she corrected. "Mr. Whittier did."

"Whittier didn't look at me with big brown eyes, turn me in the wrong direction and totally destroy what was left of my libido after almost three months of captivity."

She refused to take the blame when he was going to walk away from this with a beautiful, talented woman on his arm and she was going home to an empty Manhattan apartment.

"My parents were responsible for the color of my eyes, and probably also for my poor sense of direction. And I'm not responsible for your libido now, am I?"

She expected an angry reaction, but he remained stonily calm, his features hardening but every muscle in his body still.

"So, you're telling me I'm free to go?"

She widened her eyes at him innocently. "I have no hold on you."

"Bull," he replied succinctly. "I was a prisoner for almost three months. I know what it feels like."

"Oh, don't get righteous with me," she snapped. "You were Sylvia's prisoner long before you were mine. I saw that look in your eye when she walked into the kitchen, and I saw that kiss. How could you toy with me when you felt that way about her?"

He shifted his weight impatiently. "What you saw in my eyes was surprise. She kissed me, and it was just...a gesture between two people who'd once meant a lot to each other. Sylvia is passionate about everything. She'd worried about me while I was a hostage, and she was happy to find me free and well."

"Free." She repeated his word. "You said it yourself. You're free. Now, if you'll excuse me..."

"No, I won't." He caught her arm and pulled her back when she tried to turn toward to the house.

She tried to yank free of him, but he caught her under the arms and lifted her onto the stone wall. It was cold and wet and she protested, but he pinned her there by standing in front of her and holding a hand to the wall on each side of her.

"I know what's going on here," he said.

"So do I and I believe it's criminal," she retorted, folding her arms and hiding her bare, cold hands in the fabric of her sleeves. "Holding a woman against her will is—"

"Sometimes the only way a man can get her to listen to him," he finished for her. "If you'll just be quiet, I can be finished in a minute."

That was suddenly very desirable, because she wasn't sure she could take much more of this.

"I know you're smart enough to understand Sylvia's effusive reaction when she saw me. I think it's easier to pretend that you don't, because if you fought for me, you'd have to explain to Whittier what went on the past few days, and the national exposure of your television special is more important to you than I am." He looked into her eyes, his own grim with his apparent acceptance of what he considered a truth. "You didn't even give it a moment's serious thought, did you?"

"It looked to me," she said, angling her chin, "as though you loved her."

"It looked to me," he repeated, "as though you loved me. Goes to show you how appearances can be deceiving. You really are a phony, Liza De Lane. Your pretense goes beyond convincing everyone you're married and have children and live in the country. You want everyone to believe that your whole life is family and warmth and the spirit of Christmas all year round, when actually all you've done is *use* your family for your own purposes, and your warmth and Christmas spirit run as deep as the person you present to the television camera.''

He let that sink in and she stared at him silently, too hurt even to defend herself.

He reached for her waist, lifted her off the wall and set her on her feet. "Well, I don't need that in my life. I was a pawn in somebody else's game for almost three months and I took the chance to escape because I was sick of it. I'll be charming as hell for your big performance tonight, then I'm out of here. You can play your little games of Let's Pretend with somebody else.''

He stalked away from her toward the house.

Liza watched him go, and in the silent, snow-covered Connecticut countryside heard the crash of her whole world falling apart.

THE HEARTBEAT of the project was picking up. Liza could hear it in the busy sounds of the film crew testing their setups in the middle of the afternoon while they munched on sandwiches and fruit.

Betsy was napping and Bill and the boys had been sent upstairs to shower and dress.

Whittier followed Chris Page around like a shadow, making suggestions Chris listened to calmly then discarded as he explained patiently why they wouldn't work.

"I just want it to be really big, you know?" Whittier wheedled. "I want it to sing!"

"It's a Christmas special," Chris observed kindly. "It's going to be really big. Not because of any pretentious tricks on our part, but because of the house and Liza's angels and because of the food being prepared in the kitchen. But most of all, it's going to capture everyone's affection because of the real warmth and charm of Liza and her family. There's genuine love here, Mr. Whittier. It's going to make music without our adding the 'Hallelujah Chorus' as a background."

Whittier nodded and took the admonishment graciously. "You're right," he said. "Of course. You're right."

Liza, who'd overheard every word, wanted to scream and call a halt to everything and spill her guts. But she'd dragged everyone into this and it was now too late to back out or call it off.

And she couldn't help but believe that if Jeff didn't love Sylvia as he claimed, he'd have been more understanding of the spot she, Liza, was in.

Sherrie prepared onions for baking in a shallow pan while Liza mixed the rest of the ingredients for the Boozy Butternut Flan.

"Did you make it up with him?" Sherrie asked, taking a sip from the coffee cup that had been at her elbow all day long.

"Nope," Liza replied, taking special care with the

measuring. "He chewed me out and told me it was over."

Sherrie set the onions aside then moved to a cutting board, where she chopped onions and celery. "Smart man. Who wants a woman who isn't willing to stand up for him? To stand toe-to-toe with the woman who's trying to take him away from her and tell her where to go?"

Liza frowned at her. "Thank you, little Miss I Love Him But I Don't Want To Get Involved Again. How dare *you* tell *me* how to be in love?"

"Because you're doing such a poor job of it and I don't want you to lose him." Sherrie put the back of her wrist to her forehead and rubbed. "I'd love to have him in the family."

"You can't lose what you never had," Liza said, looking into the bowl of apricots that remained unpeeled. "It was all just a wild fantasy I was trying to play out. I mean, how often do you hear a man announce on national television that he risked his life and accomplished the impossible all because of...an image of your face?" She had to swallow to say it, and then her voice was barely there.

Sherrie stopped and turned to Liza. "Almost never," Sherrie replied. "That's why I think you should consider that this is Christmas. That God is always in the business of making miracles, but that He probably amuses Himself at Christmas by making some real stunners. And you've just been handed one."

"Could we just forget that for the time being,"

Liza pleaded, "and get this meal together? We're on the air in three hours. Shouldn't the ham be in the oven by now?"

Sherrie looked up at the kitchen clock, then back at Liza. She was pale, Liza thought, and looked just a little vague.

"Yes, it should," Sherrie said, rubbing at her forehead again. "I was thinking we had an hour more than we have. But don't worry. There's plenty of time. Help me peel these apricots."

"I insist that you stop and eat something," Liza said, reaching for a paring knife on the cutting board. Sherrie pulled the bowl of apricots between them. "Take a break. I'll get these done."

Sherrie shook her head. "No, I feel a little nauseous. You know how I am when I get nervous. If I eat anything, I'll be sick."

Liza moved her coffee cup away. "If you drink any more coffee you'll be sick. The caffeine must be burning a hole in your stomach lining by now." She went to the refrigerator and returned with a bottle of apple juice, which she poured into a glass. "Here. Have some of Betsy's beverage of choice."

Liza helped Sherrie get the ham in the oven, then spent the next hour and half under Sherrie's direction.

She tried to protest when Sherrie handed her a recipe for eggnog snow pudding.

"It's gelatin and bottled eggnog," Sherrie said. "Even you can't mess it up."

Liza glanced worriedly at her sister, knowing it

wasn't like her to put any degree of faith in Liza's cooking skills.

Chris came into the kitchen as Liza poured the pudding into cups. He frowned. "You're supposed to be in a bubble bath by now," he said, "getting ready for your big night. Come on, now. We don't need any glitches at the last minute like slacks that don't fit, or a color of sweater the camera doesn't like."

"Go." Sherrie elbowed Liza. "I'll run up when everything's ready."

Liza did as he asked, almost colliding with Bill, Jeff and the boys as they came down the stairs.

Bill and the boys were all outfitted in sweaters and cords. Jeff wore the black sweater and slacks he'd worn the day he'd arrived. She wondered how he could look even better in them than he had that day.

The boys' hair had been slicked back, making them look like perfect beings who resembled her nephews but had none of their identifying smudges and scrapes.

A makeup girl met them at the foot of the stairs and took them with her to a corner of the living room.

Davey talked the young woman's ear off as she settled him in a chair. Travis looked lovestruck.

"Took you guys long enough," Liza said, sidling between them and up the stairs, avoiding Jeff's eyes. "I'll bet I can be ready in half the time."

"Of course you can," Bill said. "You don't have to clean up the boys."

"I shouldn't have to," she said from the top of the

stairs. "I didn't talk them into helping me clean out the fireplace."

Bill looked sheepish. "I didn't think about the camera seeing inside it until Whittier pointed out that it would look dirty."

"Life is so much easier," Jeff observed, "when there aren't several million people looking in on you."

"I'm getting really anxious," Bill said, "for all this to be over."

"Amen to that." That came from Jeff.

"Oh, grumble, grumble," Liza teased airily, refusing to meet Jeff's eyes. "You're all going to love the spotlight. See you later." She hurried down the hall to Bill's room and the bathroom. She filled the tub with hot water, knowing time was short but thinking that a good twenty-minute soak would go a long way toward smoothing out her mood.

She was suffering from abject depression, overlaid by tight nerves and a complete sense of futility. She'd thought earlier that now that she knew her personal life was doomed, she'd be able to devote herself wholeheartedly to the show and what it could ultimately mean to her career.

But she didn't seem to care. She felt as though everything in her life had lost meaning. There were cheerful red guest towels with green sprigs of holly on the towel rack, and Sherrie had put a Santa-face cover on the john and a cedar wreath with gold leaves and red berries on the wall, but Liza didn't even find the picture festive.

There was no sense of celebration in her. She knew that was a circumstance she was going to have to change before airtime, because she couldn't disappoint the viewers who might be looking to her to put them in a Christmas mood when they were probably tired and stressed themselves.

But for the moment she could simply wallow in hot water filled with bubbles and think about how radically life could change in three short days.

What she feared most was that every time Christmas came around again in her future, this was what she would remember. Not the many happy Christmases past, but this one when she'd upset the lives of everyone she loved, fallen in love with a remarkable man, spent most of the night with him curled up in front of a cabin fireplace, then lost him because her lies strangled his love for her.

She closed her eyes and sank down into the suds, trying to make her mind a blank for the next fifteen minutes. The trouble was, her mind refused to cooperate. It allowed her to forget the show, to forget that she'd lied to her boss and the entire country and that she would have to explain that once the show was over.

But her mind had made a mental print of Jeff's face, and it flashed behind her eyes. She screwed her eyes shut tightly. "Go away, Jeff!" she mumbled, moving her head from side to side. "I should never have fallen for your line in the first place."

"What line?" Jeff asked.

For an instant Liza thought his image had spoken

to her and that it was growing into a full-blown hallucination.

Then she caught a whiff of his cologne and felt every nerve ending in her body flutter with awareness. She opened her eyes and saw that he was sitting on the edge of the tub, his black sweater and slacks an interesting counterpoint to the white room and the white bubbles that topped her bathwater.

His eyes looked into hers, his earlier anger replaced by a quiet neutrality.

"You feeling relaxed?" he asked.

"If only that were possible," she said, using his quiet and controlled tone. "No. I think I'll make it through the show thanks to Sherrie's expertise and my cue cards, but I will be anything but relaxed."

"I came to see if I could help with that." He stood and reached for the little wad of nylon net hanging on a hook on the shower caddy. He took a bar of clear blue soap from the rack.

Liza sat up in alarm, remembering to scoop some bubbles up with her. "What are you doing?"

"I'll scrub your back," he said as he knelt beside the tub and sloshed the nylon in the water just above her bottom. "And while I'm at it, I'll give you a back rub."

"But Sylvia wouldn't…"

"Sylvia is following Chris and Whittier around, hoping to learn something about producing a cooking show."

She looked up at him scoldingly. "And what she doesn't know won't hurt her?"

"It wouldn't hurt her if she *did* know," he said, soaping the little wad of nylon.

Resigned to her fate—and actually anticipating it—Liza drew her knees up and leaned her upper body over them to lend him access to her back.

"Why not?" she asked.

"Because she doesn't love me," he said, running the soaped puff across her shoulder blades. "But I won't go into that. It didn't interest you the first time."

"Jeff…"

"Never mind. Just concentrate on relaxing."

Right. As if she could do that with his knuckles rubbing against her bare flesh with every pass of the nylon puff, with his hand on the point of her shoulder for balance as he leaned over the edge of the tub. With him scooping up water in his hand and dropping it onto her sudsy back, then smoothing away the soap with his fingertips.

"You looked happy to see her," Liza said, despite his insistence that she relax.

"I was," he admitted. "She'll always be a good friend. Just like you'll always be a good friend."

Liza heard the softly spoken words with unutterable pain. "That's all you want from me?"

"That's all you're willing to give." He took a towel off the rack and patted her back dry with it. "You made that pretty clear. When I thought you were married, I admired you for it. Now that I know you're not, it makes me angry."

"If *you* loved *me*," she argued, "you'd be more

understanding about why I can't just blurt out that I love you until after the show. There's so much at stake for so many other people.''

''I do understand that,'' he said, tossing the towel at the closed lid of the john. His expression remained eerily free of anger or passion of any kind. He'd accepted that it was over. That was worse. ''What I don't like is that you were so ready to believe that I could chuck it all. You lied to me almost every moment of the last two days, and expected me to understand and support your motives. Then I indulge in one honest embrace with an old friend, and that somehow absolves you of the same kind of trust and support.''

''It looked like you loved her.''

''It looked like you loved Bill. Break a leg, Liza.''

He left the bathroom, pulling the door partially closed behind him.

Liza burst into tears.

THE MAKEUP GIRL WAS very upset. ''Circles I can fix,'' she scolded. ''But swollen, red eyes I can't do much about.''

''Just do your best,'' Liza encouraged briskly. ''I'll keep to the shadows.''

''With bright lights on you, you can't hide a freckle. Hold your mouth still.''

Though it was an evening show, it had been decided that Liza's makeup would be subdued and her hair caught up in a simple do in deference to the homey quality of the family Christmas.

When the makeup girl had finished, she handed Liza a mirror. "Okay?" she asked.

Liza thought she'd done brilliant work. She looked like a slightly younger, more contemporary Donna Reed, as though she took good care of her all-American-girl looks but gave up any time spent pampering them in preference to attending to her home and family.

"Wonderful," Liza said. "Thank you."

She went into the kitchen to find Sherrie still working over the baked onions. Liza remembered they took more than an hour to cook and wondered in alarm if they'd be ready in time. Then she noticed that Sherrie was still slicing apples for the cranberry-apple relish, and that the biscuit dough had yet to be cut.

Panic clutched at her.

But the room was filled with crew making last-minute adjustments to their setups, and Travis and Davey milled around among them, asking questions and serving as test subjects for lighting. Whittier stood behind a camera and looked through it at the boys to get an idea of their first inside shot.

Liza put a hand on Sherrie's shoulder, filled with guilt that she hadn't been more help to her today, and jumped back with a start when Sherrie screamed, nerves obviously at snapping point.

Sherrie spun around. The knife clattered to the floor and apple slices flew everywhere. Her face was white, her eyes enormous.

"Sis," Liza began, "you need to sit..."

But nature was already taking care of that need for her on its own. Before Liza could react, Sherrie's eyes closed slowly and her body folded gracefully to the floor.

There were gasps and shouts, then as Liza knelt beside her, pushing the knife out of the way, the boys ran to her.

Davey leaned over Sherrie and shouted plaintively, "Mom! Mom, what's the matter? Mom!" Then, his face crumpling as he understandably forgot the role he was playing, he turned to Liza and demanded, "Aunt Liza! What's wrong with my mom?"

Chapter Twelve

Bill was beside them in a moment, his mouth tight, his hands steady as he felt for a pulse.

Liza rubbed Sherrie's wrist without any real idea of what purpose it served, except that she'd often seen characters do it in old movies. "She's been working since dawn and I don't think she's taken the time to eat anything," she told Bill.

Jeff put an arm around each of the boys and drew them back while Bill sat Sherrie up and cradled her in one arm.

Bill tapped her face lightly. "Sherrie? Sherrie!"

She winced and groaned.

"What is it?" Liza demanded.

Bill ran a hand over his face in relief and sighed. "Just fainted, I think. Nerves, exhaustion, I don't know. I'd better run her into the ER to make sure."

He seemed to realize suddenly what that meant to the show. He cast her an apologetic glance as he braced Sherrie against his knee and placed an arm under her knees to lift her.

"Absolutely," she said, helping to steady Sherrie as Bill stood with her.

"I want to come," Travis said firmly.

"Me, too," Davey sobbed.

Again he looked at Liza in apology.

"Take them," Liza said, "if they won't be in the way."

"Trav, keys to the car are in my side pocket," Bill said. "I need something to cover her with."

Liza pointed to a crew member near the entrance to the dining room. "Would you get the quilt off the back of the sofa in the living room?" To the boys who were running to the back door with the keys, she shouted, "Don't forget your coats!"

The quilt was passed from hand to hand and Liza put it over Sherrie and tucked it around her. Jeff got Bill's jacket and Liza and Jeff followed him out to his car.

Sherrie came awake. "What are we doing?" she asked. "Where are we...Bill?"

"You fainted," Bill said patiently as he put her inside the front seat while Travis held the door open.

"But..." Sherrie looked around, obviously confused. "The show. Bill, the show!" She tried to push against him to get free of the seat belt he snapped into place around her.

"Stop it, Sherrie!" Liza said as Bill walked around to the driver's side, not bothering to argue with her. He let the boys into the back seat while Liza tucked the quilt around her sister. "We're going to be fine. You have everything almost done."

"No, I don't." Sherrie leaned toward Liza worriedly. "I was working in a fog the last couple of hours. It should all be done by now, but I felt..."

"Don't worry about it," Liza insisted. "Bill's taking you to the hospital to make sure you're okay."

Sherrie tried to fight off the confinement of the blanket. "I *am* okay! Liza, please!" She got a hand free and grabbed the front of Liza's sweater in a fist. "Sis, if you try to finish this dinner on your own, you're going to have the shortest TV career in the history of the tube!"

Bill turned the key in the ignition.

Liza replaced Sherrie's hand under the blanket, leaned into the car to hug her, then closed the door on her.

Liza rubbed her arms against the cold as she watched the Mercedes back out of the driveway and head for the road to town. The cold seemed somehow significant—a harbinger of what she could expect herself to be out in once the show was over.

Jeff put a fraternal arm around her shoulders. "Come on inside. If it is the shortest career in TV history, you don't want to face it with a red nose and your teeth chattering."

"I should have been more help to her today," Liza said, looking over her shoulder in the direction the car had gone.

Jeff drew her toward the house. "You tried, but everybody needed something from you today. And she seems to be pretty driven in the kitchen."

"I should have made her eat something."

"She just got busy and forgot. It was nobody's fault."

She stopped by the back door and looked up at him in surprise. "Whose side are you on, anyway?"

"Yours," he replied instantly. "Always have been."

"But you don't love me anymore." She was just trying to get things in order in her mind. The moment defied logic.

"I'll always love you," he corrected, reaching for the doorknob. "I'm just smart enough to back away from something that will never work."

He pushed the door open and Liza walked into the kitchen.

It looked as though no one had moved in the time it had taken her and Jeff to walk Bill and Sherrie and the boys out to the car.

The crew remained where they'd been standing when Davey had shattered Liza's world of illusion by leaning over Sherrie and calling her Mom. Except that someone, a young woman, was cleaning up the spilled apples.

Chris Page, headset on, clipboard in hand, stood with Whittier, whose expression was a curious combination of perplexity and horror. Liza guessed that he couldn't quite figure out what had just happened but seemed to know that it did not bode well for the show. Not well at all.

Dora, with Betsy in her arms, watched worriedly.

Liza glanced up at the kitchen clock. There were

nineteen minutes until the titles began to roll for "Christmas with Liza De Lane."

She assumed a determined stance and faced the confused crew.

"All right," she said, propping a hand on a kitchen chair for support. "I owe you an explanation. There isn't time at the moment to go into why I did this, but I imagine it's clear to you by now that the boys and Betsy are Sherrie's children and not mine. And you could probably tell by the way Bill McBride hurried to Sherrie's rescue that he's her husband and not mine. Well, he isn't yet, but he will be on New Year's Eve." She expelled a sigh because it seemed to be required to remain upright. Her broken heart and her nervous stomach felt as though they were in collusion to drive her to her knees. But it was her fault that everything had come to this point. It was her responsibility to see it through.

"But, what's worse than that," she went on, "is that my sister has all the cooking skills. All I have is the ability to write about it, and to stand in front of a camera and talk about it."

She swept a hand toward the array of half-prepared dishes covering the long kitchen counter. "The big problem is that she wasn't feeling very well, so things aren't as far along as they should be, so I don't think I'll have a finished meal for those last few minutes of the show.

"But, if you'll bear with me, I'll try to make up an excuse to the viewers and show everything as a work in progress rather than a finished meal. It won't be as effective, but it's the best I can do."

"But the opener we filmed," Chris said, "introduces your *family*. How are you going to explain that they're not here?"

"I don't know," she said calmly. "I'll think of something in time."

Chris stared at her for a moment as though she'd just stabbed him in the heart, then he turned to his crew. "Okay, people. We'll be fine for the first half. We have the intro, we have the tour of the house..." He turned to Liza with a look of sudden fear. "You can still do the tour? You can explain the decorations and..."

Liza nodded. "Yes, I can."

"Okay. And we have the angel segment just before the station break." He patted his chest right over his heart, as though it took beating his heart by hand to keep it functioning. "So we're fine until eight-thirty."

He seemed to take comfort in that as he glanced at the clock and gave a few last-minute instructions to the crew, who were suddenly spurred into action. Liza thought it strange that his nerves were soothed by the well-structured first thirty minutes. All she could think of was the impossible-to-assemble second half of the show.

She knew she was facing the death of her career. The most difficult part to deal with was the knowledge that she deserved it.

On the chance that that hadn't occurred to her, Whittier was quick to point it out.

He backed her into the far corner of the kitchen, his face pale, his eyes filled with thwarted greed. He looked deadly.

"I don't know how in the hell you intend to save your bacon, young lady," he said. "But you had damn well better, because if I fry with you, you will not be able to get a job writing *obituaries* anywhere in this country! Do I make myself clear?"

She couldn't decide if this was the real Whittier talking, or if the unbearable tension of the moment was responsible. Either way, she was toast. She smiled to herself, finding it ironic that toast was the only thing she could prepare.

"You're smiling," Whittier observed grimly. "Apparently it hasn't come home to you that whether you carry this show off or not, you're history at *Wonder Woman Magazine.*" And on the chance that that wasn't clear, he added, "Fired. Sacked. Bounced. Terminated. Stricken from the rolls!"

Panicky tears stood right behind her eyes and Liza fought them, knowing she had about five minutes to air time.

"I understand, Mr. Whittier," she said with forced dignity. "Now, speaking of rolls, I have to cut some, so if you'll excuse me..."

"I'm not through with you yet," he said, shaking a finger at her, apparently prepared to use the next five minutes to heap on more threats.

But Jeff caught him by the arm. "Yes, you are," he said. "Come on. I think Chris is hoping to fill some time by using you in the second half, and he wants to talk to you about it.''

''Oh.'' Whittier allowed himself to be drawn away, distracted from his tirade by the promise of air time.

Liza opened the utensil drawer and took out the biscuit cutter. She knew there had to be more productive things she could do at this midnight hour of preparation, but she didn't know what they were. And she did know how to cut biscuits. That was, she hoped she did.

''If we could bring in the playpen,'' Dora said, one-handedly shaking the contents of a pan on a low setting on the stove, ''I could help, but she'll scream if I put her down out of sight of us.''

Liza spared a precious instant to kiss Betsy's cheek and stroke her hair. ''Mommy's going to be fine, sweetie. Don't you worry.''

''All right, tell me what to do.''

Liza looked away from Dora and into Sylvia Stanford's face. The woman looked eager, and, more interesting than that, she looked confident.

''Sylvia, it's four minutes to air time,'' Liza demurred. ''I appreciate your offer, but I don't think...''

''Where's the menu?'' Sylvia looked around, then went to the refrigerator, where an eight-by-eleven sheet was stuck to the door with a magnet.

''The famous apricot-glazed ham. Right.'' Sylvia looked up from the sheet. ''It's in the oven?''

''Yes, but it went in late. It won't be ready in time for the—''

''Doesn't matter. We can turn up the heat so that

it's glazed and crusty on top. If we don't slice it, no one will know it isn't done inside. Baked onions…''

Liza pointed to the pan still on the counter. "They take almost an…''

Sylvia nodded, apparently knowing how long they took to bake. "Maybe we can rush them in the microwave. Cranberry-apple relish…''

Liza pointed to the apple slices still on the cutting board. "But they're oxidizing. It'll—''

"Won't matter," Sylvia said, running her finger down the list. "The cranberry will color them and it'll be beautiful. Those will be ready before the station break. Oven-browned white and sweet potatoes.''

Dora smiled. "I think I'm unnecessary," she said. "Betsy and I will see you after the show.''

Liza was beginning to feel the guillotine halt its downward slide toward her neck. "Those are peeled and in water in the refrigerator ready to go into the oven. I saw them.''

"Good. I'll put them around the ham right now. We'll get them nice and glazed looking, too, and no one will know they're still hard. Whoa. Cider pie? That's a new one on me.''

"Um." Liza tried to think. "Sherrie makes it for special occasions. It's raisins and brown sugar and all kinds of other stuff.'' She pointed to a pile of recipe cards in the corner of the counter. "All her recipes are there. Oh, Sylvia.'' She caught her by the arms at the prospect that they might be able to pull the show off after all. "Do you think you can make this work?''

"I don't know," she said honestly. "But I'll do my darnedest. You're my hero, you know."

"Opening music!" Chris called, indicating that the station was rolling titles and would soon be starting with the welcoming segment Liza had filmed earlier with Bill and the children.

"You obviously didn't hear what just happened," Liza said, starting to cut biscuits.

"You have to roll it out first, sweetie," Sylvia said, taking the cutter from her. "Finish slicing the apples, then put them in the saucepan with the cranberries. No, I didn't, but Jeff gave me a brief rundown of the last few days."

Liza sliced apples. "And you're still willing to help me. I mean, considering you...you know..."

Liza watched in astonishment as Sylvia cut biscuits with one hand, caught them in the other and put them on a pan.

Sylvia glanced up with a smile. "I'll always love Jeff, but...he told me gently but convincingly that it's not going to happen between us. And, anyway, I don't think that's what I came for. I needed to know that he was all right. And I needed some time." She kept cutting biscuits as she talked. "We just didn't shake the earth for each other." She made a face, but Liza saw a real sadness behind the attempted jocularity. "Then I met Bobby, and the earth shook so much it was all I could do to remember my name. I married him and moved to Dallas. But he wants a society wife like his mother and sisters-in-law, and that just isn't me. I have to be preparing the food, not having it served to me. So here I am.''

Liza tossed apples into the pan of cranberries.

Sylvia pointed to the refrigerator. ''Your sister's recipe calls for a can of apple juice concentrate to go in that. Then you just bring it all to a boil.''

Liza found the can, opened it and added it to the mixture. ''I'll introduce you to my boss after the show,'' Liza promised as she worked. ''My job will be open. If you're interested, I think you'll have a good shot at it. Particularly if this all works.''

Sylvia beamed.

''Liza!'' Chris shouted. ''We need you to intro Jeff! Now!''

Liza pulled off her apron and put it on Sylvia, then ran to find her spot. She felt as though her brain had been in a blender and that everything she'd ever learned was still there, but somehow liquefied. Run together. One unsortable mass of detail.

She hadn't a clue what her first line was and searched anxiously for the cue card girl. She was there with an encouraging smile.

The segment was scheduled right after a commercial and began with a news clip of Father Chabot being interviewed by a reporter and hailing Jeff as a hero and the man who'd saved his life. Then Liza was on live to introduce Jeff to the viewing audience.

She sat on the sofa and described Jeff and Father Chabot's six-day ordeal.

''And now, as our Christmas gift to you,'' she said,

"we'd like you to meet our holiday houseguest, Jeffrey James. Jeff?"

Jeff walked into the room and came toward the sofa. Liza extended her hand and he took it as the script required. Miraculously, her brain clicked on and seemed to remember what it had to do.

She asked him the questions on the cue cards and was amazed to find that she could concentrate on his answers. Her mind wasn't panicked over what came next.

He had the easy manner of a man at peace with himself, and while she noticed that, she refused to let herself think about it. In view of Sylvia's denial about their relationship, a wonderful new door had opened, but she might have already slammed it on her own foot.

But if she had, she didn't want to know about it until the show was over.

"I can't tell you how pleased we all were at *Wonder Woman*," she read off the cards toward the end of their exchange, smiling for the camera over the vagaries of fate, "to know that it was a Liza De Lane recipe that led you home."

He smiled for the audience. It was a sweet, endearing smile, she noticed. "I've corrected you on that a few times since I've been here, and, even though Bill is at the hospital tonight with a patient instead of home with us, I think your viewing audience is sufficient chaperon for me to say that *you* brought me home. You embodied for me the warmth and the spirit of family holidays, and though I had no one to come home to, you made me believe that love is there for all of us.''

Liza was speechless for a moment. That response had not been in the script. They were supposed to banter about the ham and that would allow her to plug the second half of the show filled with her recipes, and then they would go to commercial.

When she continued to stare at him, he turned to the camera and smiled. ''I believe we're going to a commercial break, and when we come back you'll have the privilege of seeing the wonderful Christmas decorations in this great old Federal mansion. We're all so lucky to have been invited here.''

''Yes!'' Chris said triumphantly when the station told him they were on break. ''Good save, Jeff. Liza, come with me. And try to wake up, honey. You're doing well, but you're a little too ethereal for prime time. Come on. We're starting by the fireplace.''

The crafts portion of the show went beautifully. ''My sister, Sherrie, decorated the house,'' she explained as they began the tour. ''We wanted you to see how natural things—holly, cedar, juniper—bring the outdoors into your home any time of the year, but particularly for the holidays when we share with nature the miracle of Christmas.''

She showed the garlands, the wreaths, the table decorations made with the most unlikely combinations, like the roses and the radishes in the kitchen.

The camera featured Sherrie's quilts strewn throughout the house, the wreaths on every door—particularly the one made of old toys on the boys' bedroom door—the candles on bedside tables, the wa-ter jug filled with holly in the dry sink in Bill's room.

In the kitchen she showed off all the possibilities for centerpieces, the wreath made of basil and straw-flowers on the open cupboard door, and the garland made of fruit and vegetables above the fireplace.

"Now stay with us," she encouraged, "and learn to make a special angel Sherrie and I have designed to share your Christmas with you."

"Okay," Chris said, "film's rolling. Now we've got about six minutes including the station break to get our act together in the kitchen." He sighed heavily. "Is there a chance?"

"Sylvia's taken over the kitchen," Liza said, lead-ing the way in while cameras moved around and the crew cast wary looks at each other—expecting the worst, she was sure, of the next half hour.

Whittier had been called into service in the kitchen and was arranging rolls in a basket lined with a lace-trimmed serviette.

"How's it going in here, Mr. Whittier?" Chris asked hopefully.

"Better than we have any right to expect," he re-plied, indicating a flushed and bright-eyed Sylvia painting glaze on a still-anemic-looking ham and po-tatoes.

"We're almost there," she said, closing the oven door on the ham and checking something in the mi-crowave. "Cranberry-apple relish is done, baked on-ions will be by the time we get to them. I started the cider pie in the microwave and baked the piecrust by itself, so by the time we combine the two it ought to look as though they were baked together and almost done. Rolls are ready, we're in the middle of broccoli with pimiento butter, but we had to scratch the corn stuffing balls unless Liza would like to show the ingredients and describe what they'll look like.''

Liza wrapped her arms around her. ''Thank you,'' she said. ''I don't deserve you. You fell out of the sky today like a miracle.''

Sylvia hugged her in return. ''I don't think many of us deserve our miracles, and yet we get them. It's Christmas. I'm glad I could help.''

''Two minutes to air!'' someone shouted.

Liza looked around for Jeff, but couldn't find him. She wondered if that would be the pattern for the rest of her life.

Sylvia was a perfect working companion. She was there with the right dish every time Liza asked for it and could contribute tips on it without taking over, though by that time Liza would have been grateful to let it be the ''Christmas with Sylvia Stanford'' show.

''I'd like you all to meet Sylvia Stanford,'' she told the camera as Sylvia showed off the cranberry-apple relish, which she'd transferred to a beautiful fluted bowl. ''As you know from the interview you saw earlier, she's a friend of Jeffrey James, and stopped by to visit today. She was conscripted into service when my...my husband was called away suddenly and a few other details of our day were changed at the last moment.''

They did fill time with the recipe for the corn stuffing balls, and Sylvia showed how to scoop them with an ice cream scoop, then added with a grin, "If you're one of those cooks who likes to save her acrylic nails."

They showed off the ham and potatoes, which Sylvia had managed to glaze beautifully so that they appeared as finished as though they'd had the extra hour to bake, then Sylvia checked the cider pie and announced regretfully that it wasn't done.

"Well, it might be when we come back," Liza said. "Stay with us for pie and flaming punch, then we'll invite you to join us for carols."

The moment Chris said they were off the air Liza turned to him in horror. "Carols! We're supposed to sing carols for five minutes to end the show! If there's anything I do worse than cook, it's sing!" She turned to Sylvia with desperation in her eyes. "Tell me you used to sing backup for Whitney Houston."

Sylvia shook her head apologetically. "I was thrown out of choir in the fourth grade. There's even an APB out on me at karaoke bars."

Liza groaned and sank into a kitchen chair. She had to face it. This show, though it was turning out miraculously glitch free, meant the end of her professional life. But having to sing alone for five minutes was bound to mean the end of her personal life, as well.

No one could possibly listen to her sing four bars of "White Christmas" and not want to kill her.

Chapter Thirteen

"Two minutes, people!" someone shouted.

Liza determined that she would find whoever owned that voice and teach him to say something else—like, "Technical difficulties! We're off the hook," or "We've been preempted by a message from the president!"

No. There was no rescue imminent. She was going to have to get through this on her own, and if she had to, she was going to sing all by herself for five interminable minutes.

She looked around for Jeff again but couldn't spot him. She wondered if he'd left, finished with her and Whittier and their entire Christmas fiasco.

The kitchen door opened a crack suddenly and Sherrie peered around it. She saw everyone running around and talking and pushed the door the rest of the way open. "Are we on a break?" she asked.

Liza ran to her, pulling her into the kitchen. Bill and the boys spilled in after her. "Are you okay? What are you doing back so soon?"

"I'm fine." Sherrie waved her away, shrugged out

of her coat and went to the food. "It was a sinking thing."

Liza frowned at Bill. "A syncopal episode," he corrected. "No real reason for it, except probably that she was hungry and edgy."

"What can I do at this point to…?" Sherrie was asking, looking around the kitchen. Then she noticed the finished dishes in the middle of the table and gasped. "What happened? You didn't do this."

It wasn't a question, it was a statement of fact. Sherrie was back.

Liza shook her head. "Sylvia finished everything. But we're not slicing anything, because she pulled a few fancy maneuvers to make things look like they're finished when they're really not."

"Wow," Sherrie breathed. "A miracle."

Liza looked at her family, at the woman who'd saved her life at the last moment, and at the wonderfully festive atmosphere of the kitchen despite all the cameras, cables and lights all over, and decided that the past few days had indeed been a miracle.

She'd met Jeff James, and, though she'd well and truly blown that opportunity, she would never forget last night in his arms in the cabin. Bill and Sherrie had solved their problems and were getting married. Sherrie would have her inn, Liza would see that Edie kept her job, and then she would use her part of the money to take a brief break and decide what to do with the rest of her life.

Somewhere the loving warmth this home exuded had to exist for her. All she had to do was find it.

And she knew she couldn't do that with dishonesty between herself and the public who looked to her for their homemaking ideas.

"All right," she said briskly, pulling chairs out at the table. "I want you all sitting around the table like dinner guests while we display the food."

"But you're supposed to..." Chris began.

Liza shook her head. "I know. But I want to do it this way."

"Liza," Whittier's voice warned.

She blew him a kiss. "You've already fired me, Mr. Whittier," she said amiably, "and threatened to leave me globally jobless. There's nothing more you can do to me at this point, except go along with whatever I want."

He opened his mouth to protest, then closed it again with a frown, apparently deciding she was right.

"Aunt Liza." Davey tugged at the hem of her sweater as he walked around her to take a chair. "I'm sorry I forgot about *you* being my mom."

She hugged him tightly, then kissed his cheek. "It doesn't matter, Davey. It was a dumb idea in the first place. But I've fixed everything."

Travis looked worried. "But Mr. Whittier fired you."

She shook her head. "Doesn't matter. I'll find something else even more fun and more exciting to do. You two did a great job and your bikes are already in the garage, so don't worry about it."

The boys squealed gleefully, guilt forgotten as they took their places.

"Okay," she said to the group around the table. "Just follow my lead."

Bill looked up at her. "Isn't that why we're in doo-doo up to our armpits already?"

Liza kissed the top of his head. "Yes, it is. So, once you're dirty, what's a little more?"

She looked toward Chris, watching for his five-second countdown, and spotted Jeff, standing behind him watching the action.

She made a frantic beckoning movement. "Jeff!" she whispered. "Come here!"

He came toward her with a look of puzzlement. "What do you...?"

"Five...four..."

"Just stay with me, okay?"

"Three..."

"I'm not singing for you, Liza," he warned.

Liza pulled him into position beside her and held for dear life on to the back of the chair at the head of the table.

The "two" and "one" were mouthed rather than spoken, and Chris counted them off on his fingers, then pointed to Liza.

This was it, she knew. The segment that would make or break her entire life—professional and personal.

"Welcome back to Christmas with Liza De Lane," she said into the camera, the tension that had eluded her during the previous segments suddenly crashing down on her full force.

She did her best to ignore it and concentrate on what she had to do.

"We've all gathered around the table to enjoy our sumptuous Christmas Eve dinner, but because my readers, and tonight, our viewing audience, have become like family to us, I want to invite you into the real world of Liza De Lane. Since we can't have you all around the table to chat, I'm asking you to pretend that my sister, Sherrie, and I are sitting with you in your homes while I tell you how the Liza De Lane column came to be."

Sherrie, seated to the right of the head of the table, looked up at her in alarm. Liza ignored her.

As clearly as her nervousness would allow her, Liza explained how she'd lost her job a year and a half ago, how Sherrie had been a single mother, and how she'd talked her into working the column with her as a silent partner. She talked with a slight tremor in her voice about how she'd never shown any skill in the kitchen, but loved to write and had always dreamed of raising a family in a home like Bill McBride's.

"Sherrie, on the other hand," she said, "has always been a genius in the kitchen and is usually too busy cooking to take the time to write about it. And she's not comfortable with speaking in front of a group of people.

"It wasn't that we ever intended to deceive you," she explained, "but because Sherrie and I have always turned to each other for what we needed, this seemed like a perfect way to combine our talents.

"Your response to us was so warming that we wanted to do more for you, and the more we did, the more you responded and soon there was no turning back."

She paused to draw a breath, hoping it would steady her. It didn't. The crew was casting nervous looks at each other, Whittier had turned his back to her and Chris was waiting in apparent agony for it to all be over.

But she owed her audience the truth, and her sister some recognition.

"So, when the opportunity came to do tonight's show in my home and with my family," she went on intrepidly, "I didn't want to disappoint all of you by showing you around my Manhattan apartment, and introducing you to my goldfish. So I talked Sherrie into letting me borrow *her* family."

She could almost hear the collective gasp across America.

"Travis, Davey and Betsy—" Liza indicated them and saw Chris point to a camera to focus on them "—are really Sherrie's children. And Bill..." She reached a hand out to touch Bill's shoulder. The camera moved in his direction. "Is really Sherrie's fiancé. He *is* a pediatrician here in Rockbury, though. That part was true. He agreed to help me because he loves Sherrie." She smiled, imagining a receptive response from her audience, refusing to think that they'd already shut off their televisions and were throwing their *Wonder Woman* magazines into the fire.

She went to stand behind her sister's chair. The

camera moved to focus on her. "And this is Sherrie, my sister, my friend and the chef at the Rockbury Inn in town. She's been there every time I needed her, and all the column's recipes and household hints came from her. She decorated Bill's house for Christmas, planned and prepared this wonderful menu, then ended up in the hospital just before our show began because she worked too hard and forgot to eat."

Liza reached a hand off-camera for Sylvia and drew her into the picture. "I thought I was doomed, that I was going to have to admit to you at the beginning of the show what I'd done and beg your indulgence while I read Christmas cards or played Christmas CDs. But Sylvia is an old friend of Jeff's, who showed up this morning to welcome him home. She stepped in to finish what Sherrie had begun for me." Liza pulled out a chair for her near the end of the table and encouraged her to sit. "I guess the point of all this is that without the support of my family and friends, I'm no one special. But with it...well, here we are."

She went back to Jeff, trying desperately to read what was in his eyes. They watched her with dark intensity, but she couldn't tell if they showed approval or condemnation for her on-air confession.

She hooked her arm in his and saw Chris gesture the cameraman to move in for a close-up. "And something remarkable has happened to Jeff James and me over the last few days. He says that the image of me in his mind is what helped him get home. Well..." She turned to look into his eyes. "His image has lived in my mind since I was a very young girl, putting together my notion of the perfect life's mate. He is home. We're going to be married before the New Year."

This time she did hear the collective gasp—at least, from that small fraction of the country collected around her table and over mikes and cameras in her kitchen.

Jeff didn't move or speak, but she felt the tightening of the arm she held.

"I think love is always the strongest force in the universe. But at Christmas, when it was truly born, it ignites in all of us. It led Jeff home, it flows from Sherrie to me to everyone gathered around our table, and tonight it lives in this house in Connecticut. I wish you could be here to share it with us, but since you can't, we send it out to you with full hearts."

All right. She'd said everything she'd intended to say. Sherrie and Sylvia were crying, but it was impossible to tell what Jeff thought.

Chris Page was clearly worried about the next five minutes of the show. He kept making a stretching motion and pointing to the book of carols he held in his hand.

Liza had no idea how she got through the next five minutes. Luckily, the boys were enthused about singing and helped carry the reluctant adults' first tentative bars of "Away in a Manger."

By the time they moved on to "We Three Kings," the crew had joined in and they were beginning to sound to Liza's ear like the Mormon Tabernacle Choir.

Soon it was time to say good-night. Chris silently encouraged the group to keep singing, but made a quieting motion with his hands.

Raising her voice, Liza focused on the light on the camera. "From Rockbury, Connecticut, to every corner of our world, Merry Christmas from my family to each and every one of you. And we wish you all the love and warmth we share tonight."

She blew a kiss and—mercifully—Chris yelled, "Yes! That's a wrap! We did it. We actually *did* it!"

There were shouts and applause from the crew, but Whittier stepped out in front of them, his severe expression dampening and finally stopping their excitement.

"You told the whole world," he said, pointing his finger at Liza, "that *Wonder Woman Magazine* is a liar. And you didn't have to. Sylvia here saved us, but that wasn't good enough. You had to grandstand! I'm taking you before a judge, young lady, and suing you for..."

Bill pushed himself away from the table, but Jeff stopped him with a hand on his shoulder. "You're the make-believe husband, remember? I'll handle this." He left Liza's side to confront Whittier.

"You consider being honest grandstanding because you wouldn't know an honest thought if it fell on your head from a twelfth-story window! You never do anything without an eye to how it's going to affect your corporation's bank balance. You don't give a damn about Liza, just about what she does for your circulation. And you never cared a rip about me except in as far as I might plump up your audience.''

Jeff leaned a little closer. Whittier took a step back. ''And don't you ever raise your voice to her again, or you'll find yourself without one.''

Liza listened in disbelief. Then Jeff rounded on her and she realized quickly that he might be on her side, as he'd admitted earlier that day, but that didn't mean he intended to remain in her life. The dark snap in his eyes didn't look at all like the expression of a loving man who was thrilled that she'd introduced him to millions of viewers as her fiancé.

But before anyone could say anything more, a loud commotion could be heard coming from the living room.

''I waited until you wrapped!'' an angry male voice shouted. ''Now I want to see her, or there'll be bodies from here to Texas. Let me through!''

''Oh-oh,'' Sylvia said ominously.

Jeff turned to face the intruder and Bill went to stand beside him.

Liza was not surprised to see a tall cowboy storm through the dining room and to the edge of the kitchen where Jeff and Bill stood as a barrier to his entrance. The loud voice had had the lilt of Texas to it.

The man wore a Western-cut sports jacket in gray over leg-hugging gray slacks. Liza saw a white dress shirt under the jacket, and a white silk scarf around his neck, both ends of it dangling over a formidable chest. He held a gray Stetson in one hand. He was about Bill's age and seemed as vital.

He took one look at Jeff and Bill and stopped. It didn't seem to be fear in his eyes, but a sort of resigned acceptance.

"Gentlemen," he said, looking from one to the other, "I don't mean anyone any harm. My wife ran away yesterday without a goodbye, and I've come a long way to get her back. Now, would you please let me through?"

"Women don't usually run away from men they enjoy being with," Bill said quietly.

"Unless they're Sylvia Stanford Hickock," the cowboy said. "Then the rules of reason don't apply. When she thinks she's not getting enough attention, she does things for effect." The man's eyes narrowed on Jeff. "Jeff James?" he asked.

"Yes," Jeff replied.

The cowboy smiled thinly. "Then you should know what I'm talking about. I'm Bobby Hickock, Sylvia's husband."

He and Jeff shook hands.

"I was busy with a merger," Bobby said. "And I did sort of...forget...that it was Christmas."

Sylvia pushed her way between Jeff and Bill and glowered up at her husband. "You don't want me to work, so that I can be home when you're home, but you never *come* home, and I won't put my life on hold indefinitely while you buy up the country and spend all your time rearranging it."

"Okay," he said. Liza saw his eyes devour Sylvia's face, as though twenty-four hours without her had been far too long. "You're right. I'm new at being married. I have a lot to learn."

Sylvia's shoulders sagged, all the wind apparently knocked out of her by that admission.

She folded her arms. "I'm considering going into television," she said. "With a cooking show."

He took that news with equanimity, then looked around at all the equipment filling the kitchen and asked with a wince, "Is the ranch going to look like this every day?"

"No," she said. "I'd do that part in a studio."

He spread both hands. "Then, fine."

She firmed her jaw. "I'm not your mother or your sisters-in-law. I'm *me*."

He glanced at Bill and Jeff as though sure that was a declaration they'd heard before.

"You certainly are," he said. "Fine. Now, are you coming home?"

She folded her arms. "I don't know. Maybe it'd be better for us to spend some time ap—"

That was as far as she got before he put his shoulder to her waist and lifted her off the floor.

She put a hand over her eyes as she dangled over his back. Then she raised her head and focused on Liza and Sherrie. "What *is* it about self-confident men that we find attractive?"

Sherrie laughed. "It isn't the self-confidence. It's all the other good stuff that comes with it, so we put up with the authoritative attitude."

The crew parted as Bobby walked with Sylvia to

the door. Liza ran ahead for Sylvia's coat and handed it to Bobby, who slung it over his free arm.

"Thank these nice people for their hospitality," he said.

Sylvia lifted her head to smile at all of them, then focused on Jeff. "Be happy," she said.

He nodded. "I have every intention of doing so. You, too. Merry Christmas."

Everyone gathered on the porch to wave them off, then the crew hurriedly packed their things to get home in time for their own family Christmas Eves.

As Liza turned to lend a hand, Jeff caught her arm. "Excuse us for a few minutes," he said with a glance at Bill, then at Sherrie. "We need a little private time to talk."

"Sure." Sherrie smiled widely. "I'll see what I can do about finishing up the meal. We might actually be able to eat it by the time you come down. But now that everyone's leaving, the kids are going to be antsy about their presents, so don't take too long."

"Half an hour," Jeff said. "Tops."

"Good."

Jeff led Liza up the stairs, into the bedroom he'd occupied since his arrival, then closed and locked the door.

The room was cool and dark, and snow drifted silently beyond the window.

The subtle sounds of packing up could be heard from downstairs.

Jeff pulled Liza to the side of the bed and sat her down. He sat beside her on his bent knee so that he could face her. "Fiancé?" he asked, a note of impatience in his voice.

Oh, God. He wasn't really on her side, he'd just wanted to oppose Whittier. He was angry that she'd introduced him as her fiancé.

Since it was a night for honesty, she angled her chin and decided to go all the way. "Fiancé," she repeated. "This whole thing began because all I was really doing was putting my dreams on paper. Tonight, of course, I was putting them on the air. And marrying you has become the center of...all my...dreams." She sighed and prayed for yet another miracle. "And introducing a man in front of millions of people as the one you intend to marry kind of forces him into stopping to think, doesn't it? I mean, if you walk away from me now because I lied to you, you'll only regret it later when you miss me and realize that I lied because I wanted so much to meet you, and that I continued to lie because I'd fallen in love with you."

He was horrifyingly silent for what seemed an eternity. "Or, I could be wrong," she admitted wearily. "I noticed you were missing for some time." She pointed to the suitcase on the chair. "Did you come up to pack?"

"No." He studied her face feature by feature, then looked into her eyes. "Actually, I was calling the man who owns the cabin and the barn where we spent last night."

She blinked. "Why?"

"Because," he said gravely, "I think Whittier was

right. You should be taken before a judge. Only, I'm going to do it.''

Breathless and confused, she parted her lips to ask him why, but couldn't.

He smiled. ''To marry you,'' he said, pulling her into his arms and kissing her soundly. When he drew away again his smile was tender. ''Then to get the permits required to add on to the cabin and renovate the barn. Architecture isn't exactly engineering, but it's close enough. So, what do you say? You want to stay here and design and build a house, a few kids, the kind of home you've always dreamed about, so that you have something honest to say in your column this time around?''

Liza stared at him, speechless. It was happening. Her own personal miracle. She'd created a wonderful fictitious world and God was making it real for Christmas.

''I'll take that as a yes,'' Jeff said, and opened his mouth over her parted lips.

It was the kiss they'd never had the opportunity to share, filled with all the feelings they'd hidden, first because she was supposed to be married, then later—because she wasn't.

His hands molded her to him, stroking her back, her waist, her hip.

Her fingertips explored his shoulders, his warm, solid chest concealed by the sweater, and stopped to feel his heartbeat. It pulsed against her palm, strong and steady.

He nipped at her bottom lip. ''It beats for you,''

he whispered. "I can't believe that I dreamed of you all those weeks and now..." He tipped his head back to look at her in wonder. "You're mine."

Her eyes, she was sure, reflected the same amazement. "I took one look at you on television and...I *knew* you were mine. But who would ever believe—"

Her question was interrupted by a loud rap on the door.

"Liza? Jeff!" It was Whittier's voice.

Liza groaned and leaned her head against Jeff's shoulder. "Don't answer," she whispered.

"I—I know you're in there!" Whittier's voice sounded jovial. Liza raised her head to look at Jeff suspiciously.

"You won't believe what's happened!" Whittier said. "The station's getting calls from all over the country! Nobody seemed to notice that you've been tricking them for a year and a half, Liza. All they heard was that the darling of country living is marrying the hero of the moment!"

Jeff rolled his eyes.

Liza kissed him. "You'll be my hero forever!" she whispered.

He returned the kiss slowly and artfully as Whittier went on. "So...I may have been...hasty in firing you. In fact, I'd like to make up for that by doubling your salary and promising you two specials next year! Liza! What do you say? Liza? Jeff! You wouldn't want her to pass up an opportunity like that? Oh! And my agent's working on a book deal for you!"

Jeff raised his head. "I can't write," he whispered to Liza.

"Not a problem," she replied. "I can."

"We'll call you," Jeff said, raising his voice to be heard on the other side of the door, "when we get back from the honeymoon." Then he tipped Liza onto her back on the coverlet and braced himself over her on his forearms.

"Merry Christmas, my love," he said.

"Merry Christmas, darling," she replied.

"Guys?" Whittier called. "When will that be? Jeff? Liza?"

He didn't get an answer.

A HOLIDAY RECIPE FROM THE KITCHEN OF
Muriel Jensen

When I was growing up, my parents' little
apartment was filled with the wonderful aromas
of Portuguese sausage cooking, or tourtière
baking—a French-Canadian pork pie sort of
thing—and all kinds of other goodies we ate
mostly at holiday time. Hope you enjoy
this taste of our family Christmas!

TOURTIÈRE

1 lb lean pork
1 tsp salt
1/2 tsp pepper
1/4 tsp each ground cloves, cinnamon and marjoram
2 tsp cornstarch
1 cup water
pastry for 2 crust, 8-inch pie

Combine all ingredients (except pastry). Simmer,
covered, for 30 minutes, stirring frequently. Line
pie pan with one crust pastry, pour meat mixture
into it, top with second crust and crimp edges
together. Prick with fork. Bake at 425°F for 10
minutes. Reduce heat to 350°F and bake for
35 minutes longer, until top crust is golden. Makes
six servings.

Every month there's another title from one
of your favorite authors!

October 1997
Romeo in the Rain by Kasey Michaels
When Courtney Blackmun's daughter brought home Mr. Tall,
Dark and Handsome, Courtney wanted to send the young
matchmaker to her room! Of course, that meant the single
New Jersey mom would be left alone with the irresistibly
attractive Adam Richardson....

November 1997
Intrusive Man by Lass Small
Indiana's Hannah Calhoun had enough on her hands taking
care of her young son, and the last thing she needed was a
man complicating things—especially Max Simmons, the
gorgeous cop who had eased himself right into her little boy's
heart…and was making his way into hers.

December 1997
Crazy Like a Fox by Anne Stuart
Moving in with her deceased husband's—*eccentric*—family
in Louisiana meant a whole new life for Margaret Jaffrey and
her nine-year-old daughter. But the beautiful young widow
soon finds herself seduced by the slower pace and the much-
too-attractive cousin-in-law, Peter Andrew Jaffrey....

**BORN IN THE USA: Love, marriage—
and the pursuit of family!**

Available at your favorite retail outlet!

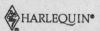 

BUSA3

Once upon a time…

We were little girls dreaming of
handsome princes on white chargers…of
fairy godmothers…and of mountain castles
where we'd live happily ever after.

Now that we're all grown up,
Harlequin American Romance lets us
recapture those dreams in a miniseries
aimed at the little girl who still
lives on inside of us. Join us for stories
based on some of the world's best-loved
fairy tales in

Once Upon a Kiss…

Look for the next magical fairy-tale romance:

DADDY & THE MERMAID
by Charlotte Maclay
Available in January 1998

Once Upon a Kiss… At the heart of every
little girl's dream…and every woman's fantasy…

HFAIRY6

DEBBIE MACOMBER

invites you to the

HEART·OF·TEXAS

Join Debbie Macomber as she brings you the lives
and loves of the folks in the ranching community
of Promise, Texas.

If you loved Midnight Sons—don't miss
Heart of Texas! A brand-new six-book series
from Debbie Macomber.

Available in February 1998
at your favorite retail store.

Heart of Texas by Debbie Macomber

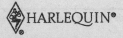
HARLEQUIN®

HPHRT1

**Don't miss these Harlequin favorites
by some of our bestselling authors! Act now and
receive a discount by ordering two or more titles!**

HT#25720	A NIGHT TO REMEMBER	$3.50 U.S.	☐
	by Gina Wilkins	$3.99 CAN.	
HT#25722	CHANGE OF HEART	$3.50 U.S.	☐
	by Janice Kaiser	$3.99 CAN.	
HP#11797	A WOMAN OF PASSION	$3.50 U.S.	☐
	by Anne Mather	$3.99 CAN.	
HP#11863	ONE-MAN WOMAN	$3.50 U.S.	☐
	by Carole Mortimer	$3.99 CAN.	
HR#03356	BACHELOR'S FAMILY	$2.99 U.S.	☐
	by Jessica Steele	$3.50 CAN.	
HR#03441	RUNAWAY HONEYMOON	$3.25 U.S.	☐
	by Ruth Jean Dale	$3.75 CAN.	
HS#70715	BAREFOOT IN THE GRASS	$3.99 U.S.	☐
	by Judith Arnold	$4.50 CAN.	
HS#70729	ANOTHER MAN'S CHILD	$3.99 U.S.	☐
	by Tara Taylor Quinn	$4.50 CAN.	
HI#22361	LUCKY DEVIL	$3.75 U.S.	☐
	by Patricia Rosemoor	$4.25 CAN.	
HI#22379	PASSION IN THE FIRST DEGREE	$3.75 U.S.	☐
	by Carla Cassidy	$4.25 CAN.	
HAR#16638	LIKE FATHER, LIKE SON	$3.75 U.S.	☐
	by Mollie Molay	$4.25 CAN.	
HAR#16663	ADAM'S KISS	$3.75 U.S.	☐
	by Mindy Neff	$4.25 CAN.	
HH#28937	GABRIEL'S LADY	$4.99 U.S.	☐
	by Ana Seymour	$5.99 CAN.	
HH#28941	GIFT OF THE HEART	$4.99 U.S.	☐
	by Miranda Jarrett	$5.99 CAN.	

(limited quantities available on certain titles)

TOTAL AMOUNT	$	_____
DEDUCT: 10% DISCOUNT FOR 2+ BOOKS	$	_____
POSTAGE & HANDLING	$	_____
($1.00 for one book, 50¢ for each additional)		
APPLICABLE TAXES*	$	_____
TOTAL PAYABLE	$	_____

(check or money order—please do not send cash)

To order, complete this form and send it, along with a check or money order for the
total above, payable to Harlequin Books, to: **In the U.S.:** 3010 Walden Avenue, P.O. Box
9047, Buffalo, NY 14269-9047; **In Canada:** P.O. Box 613, Fort Erie, Ontario, L2A 5X3.

Name: _____

Address: _____ City: _____

State/Prov.: _____ Zip/Postal Code: _____

*New York residents remit applicable sales taxes.
Canadian residents remit applicable GST and provincial taxes.

HBKOD97

He's every woman's fantasy, but only one woman's dream come true.

For the first time Harlequin American Romance brings you THE ULTIMATE...in romance, pursuit and seduction—our most sumptuous series ever. Because wealth, looks and a bod are nothing without that one special woman.

THE ULTIMATE...

Pursuit

They're

#711 ~~SHE'S~~ THE ONE! by Mindy Neff
January 1998

Stud

#715 HOUSE HUSBAND by Linda Cajio
February 1998

Seduction

#723 HER PRINCE CHARMING by Nikki Rivers
April 1998

Catch

#729 MASQUERADE by Mary Anne Wilson
June 1998

The romance continues in four spin-off books.

Discover what destiny has in store when Lina, Arianna, Briana and Molly crack open their fortune cookies!

PAIN CAN BE THE MIDWIFE OF JOY

THIS CHILD IS MINE
Janice Kaiser
Superromance #761
October 1997

NEVER JUDGE A BOOK BY ITS COVER

DOUBLE TAKE
Janice Kaiser
Temptation #659
November 1997

DISCOVER YOUR DREAMS AND DISCOVER YOURSELF

THE DREAM WEDDING
M.J. Rodgers
Intrigue #445
December 1997

FOLLOW YOUR DREAM

JOE'S GIRL
Margaret St. George
American Romance #710
January 1998

Available wherever Harlequin books are sold.